LETTERS FROM LONDON
AND EUROPE

℘

"The unstated theme of these extraordinary letters is death;
not just the death of an aristocracy or a redundant way of
life, but more broadly of Sicily – and of Europe."
Ian Thomson, *The Financial Times*

"There are pleasures on every page of these sparkling letters."
The Scotsman

"We should be grateful for the letters that, having survived and
been translated into English, paint a vivid picture of the country
Lampedusa would have loved to call his own." *Standpoint*

"This selection of [Lampedusa's] letters… gathers much
brilliantly atmospheric writing from the future novelist, who
embellishes as much as he reports." *The Independent*

"An attractive and nicely translated volume… this
correspondence… is important because it illuminates the decade
of Lampedusa's life about which least had been known."
David Gilmour, *TLS*

"*Letters from London and Europe* usefully illuminates
[Lampedusa's] Anglophilia, shows him at epistolary play, and
gets a little behind his perpetual guardedness… an enterprising
publication." Julian Barnes, *The Guardian*

"The letters of Giuseppe Tomasi di Lampedusa… showcase
a love of the physical, and a keen wit and intelligence in the
author of *The Leopard*." *The Daily Telegraph*

LETTERS
FROM LONDON
AND EUROPE
(1925–30)

GIUSEPPE TOMASI
DI LAMPEDUSA

Edited by Gioacchino Lanza Tomasi
and Salvatore Silvano Nigro

Translated by J.G. Nichols

Foreword by Francesco da Mosto

ALMA BOOKS

ALMA BOOKS LTD
London House
243–253 Lower Mortlake Road
Richmond
Surrey TW9 2LL
United Kingdom
www.almabooks.com

First published in Italian as *Viaggio in Europa*
by Arnoldo Mondadori Editore in 2006
English translation first published by Alma Books Ltd in 2010
This paperback edition with new additional material first published in 2011

This book is published with the support of the Italian Ministry of Foreign Affairs

Supported by the National Lottery through Arts Council England

LOTTERY FUNDED

Printed in Great Britain by CPI Cox & Wyman Ltd, Reading

ISBN: 978-1-84688-137-4

CONTENTS

Foreword

Francesco da Mosto

To write about these letters by Giuseppe Tomasi di Lampe-dusa, I cannot help but immerse myself in that world which, on my mother's side, I half-belong to. It is an insular world. It is the world of Sicily, which Lampedusa defines as "the Iceland of the South" or the "Island of Fire" – and it is the world of Palermo and the Conca d'Oro, which he describes in infernal, Dantesque terms: "a large town, low-lying and red-hot, enclosed in a circle of steel-grey cliffs, the whole enveloped in a great cloud of reddish dust".

Being half from the island of Sicily and half from that of Venice, I realize that we islanders are odd people, even eccentric, with an inborn need to cook up something – whatever it may be – as long as it's original. In the Palermo of last century, there were even people who had funerals for their cats, or had the *Corriere della Sera* publish an obituary for their pet blackbird.

I cannot remember the first time I went to Palermo, and it seems as if I have always been on my way there – I have always felt that dry heat and seen the reddish dust covering the paving stones of the doorway. The sand comes from the Sahara, which the sirocco blows over all the way from Africa, as I was told every year, always unsure whether to believe it or not, yet dreaming of clouds of sand in the sky.

My mother was born in Palermo, and she lived there until she got married. So every year, for Christmas, we went down to visit the grandparents, aunts and uncles, cousins and the whole extended family. All of them belonged to the Bellini Club, just like Lampedusa and his cousins, the Piccolos, to whom most of these letters are addressed.

My grandfather remembered Lampedusa from his times at the Bellini and the various balls, where he often leant against the door jamb, like a spectator rather than an actor in that magical comedy, together with Roberto Lucchesi Palli, Duca della Grazia. As a result, the pair received the nickname of "The Pillars of Hercules".

At the time, it was common for the Sicilian aristocracy to travel regularly to France and England. In Paris, the ladies would get fitted from head to toe, while the men went to London to get custom-made shirts and shoes, and stopped in Paris for the gibus, the collapsible top hat. We used my grandfather's as an accordion or – walking with a bone-topped cane in arm – lowered it over our eyes to imitate him.

Among the "travelling" Bellini members, my grand-father Ciccio sent his shirts to London to be laundered. Another member, Cicciuzzo, the "Demented", from the landowning family of the Cupane barons, was extremely intelligent and had an almost maniacal taste for paradox. He would come out of the library with his clothes all crumpled, exclaiming: "I went on the most marvellous trip – I've just come back from China" – and asking the Maestro di Casa, before leaving the Club, to send home a telegram with instructions to wake him up the next morning. Slovenly and always with unkempt hair and beard, he was very different from his cousin Cicciuzzo, the "Lackey", who always looked like a true gentleman, perfectly turned out and well dressed.

Other members of my Sicilian family travelled too, also in very eccentric ways. One of my uncle's ancestors had vowed to make a pilgrimage to the Holy Land if he survived a cholera epidemic, but since he didn't have enough money to embark on such a long journey, he decided to replicate the expedition through his garden and inside his own house. So, on a Monday night, he set off for the "Holy Land" with his butler: one day they would camp near the fish pond, where the papyrus plants would brush against the fabric of the tent; another day in the flower bed under the orange-tree blossoms; one day in the stables, and the next in the ballroom or the music room, covering the whole distance until they finally reached their destination. To celebrate their arrival, a mass was held in the house chapel, after which my uncle's ancestor turned to the butler and said: "And now let's get ready for the journey home." To which the butler is said to have replied, in a deferential tone, "M'Lord, if you don't mind, I'd rather stay here, in the Holy Land."

In the years between 1925 and 1930, the future author of *The Leopard,* then in his thirties, also travelled a great deal, especially in Europe, reaching as far as the Baltic. He would leave Palermo at the beginning of the summer, and return well into the autumn, after long stays in his beloved England and in Paris, and often also in Germany. Then he would cross Austria, sometimes going on to Latvia, finally to return to Sicily via Switzerland or the Alto Adige region.

In these *Letters from London and Europe* – part sketch-writing and part burlesque entertainment – we can already glimpse a hint of the sort of writing we will find in *The Leopard*. With the precision of a great narrator, Lampedusa gives detailed descriptions of the landscape and the people he meets, mostly referring to himself in the third person – a solitary traveller who perceives the world around him in a fairly detached way. It is a way of writing and being that is undoubtedly intrinsic to Lampedusa's character and upbringing, but which is also in some ways influenced and inspired by his roots – that Sicilian world which, perhaps because it is an island, leaves its distinctive and picturesque trace.

Lampedusa's letters are full of jokes, puns, witticisms, grotesque exaggerations, allusions and literary references – all things which his correspondents, the Piccolo brothers, would have fully understood and appreciated. Of course, one cannot help but notice the occasional cutting remark about Jewish people, or his superficial views on the advance of Fascism. These are elements which unfortunately were, in Lampedusa's time and circle, fairly common. But it is hardly an ideological judgement on his part – rather a sceptical, crude glance at the outside world.

All in all these letters, like Lampedusa's masterpiece, *The Leopard*, in which the actors are members of the family, are a faithful, ironic and paradoxical description of life itself – whether tragic or comic.

Introduction

Gioacchino Lanza Tomasi

The correspondence of Giuseppe Tomasi di Lampedusa, as preserved by his heirs, consists of two main collections. The most substantial group, which is not included in the present volume and is currently being prepared for publication, is made up of the letters between the married couple. Giuseppe and his wife, Alessandra Wolff Stomersee, exchanged a very large number of letters: about four hundred of them survive. They have come down to us in groups of letters from one spouse to the other; but the two series seldom intersect, and therefore the interlinking coming and going of the correspondence has been lost. These letters, often sent at the rate of three per week, must have been at least twice as many in total, considering the replies are almost always missing. They are all in French, and are characterized by an inconsistent flow of information: the rapport between the spouses would have suffered if it had been too detailed: hence the exchange reflects a relationship which was close and at the same time circumspect (on his part).

The second group consists of about seventy letters sent to Italian correspondents, some of whom were the writer's best friends. Among these, there is a particular biographical importance for the understanding of the distinctive personality of Lampedusa before 1955 – the year in which my direct testimony and that of my contemporaries begins – in the letters to two friends whom he met in the prison camp: Guido Lajolo and Bruno Revel. These letters are few – three to Revel and three to Lajolo – but in contrast to the others they are utterly frank, and in them one finds that the correspondents are on the same wavelength. In 2010 Ilaria Erede, granddaughter of Massimo Erede, another fellow prisoner of Lampedusa in Szombathely, wrote her BA dissertation based on twenty-three items – postcards and letters – addressed by Lampedusa to her grandfather. With her father's permission, these are now added in the Appendix to the present edition. In the Twenties, Massimo Erede played an important role in Lampedusa's life. Through him he got in touch with Mario Maria Martini, a wealthy man and the editor of the literary monthly *Le Opere e i Giorni*. Lampedusa, under the name Giuseppe Tomasi di Palma, contributed to the monthly in 1926 with two essays on Paul Morand and W.B. Yeats. In 1927 he published a longer essay, which was printed in two successive numbers of the magazine. It is a review of Richard Gundolf's *Caesar: Geschichte seines Ruhms*. Obviously all the letters to Italian correspondents are in Italian, and therefore in a language of which Lampedusa, in contrast with French, was totally in command.

The bulk of the letters given in this volume, acquired by the Fondazione Biblioteca di via Senato of Milan, are addressed to the Piccolo cousins of Calanovella and represent a crucial discovery for the understanding of Lampedusa in the five years from 1925 to 1930. To the letters which make up this pool are added here two others, to make a total of twenty-nine: one (V) to Casimiro Piccolo, preserved in the archives of the Fondazione Famiglia Piccolo di Calanovella at Capo d'Orlando, the other (XXVII) to Aunt Alice Barbi, the wife of Pietro Tomasi della Torretta, preserved by Lampedusa's heirs and given here because of its chronological and thematic affinity.

In the Appendix, besides the recently discovered items addressed to Massimo Erede, there are three more letters. The first one, held by Lampedusa's heirs, was sent to the author by his mother when he was in London on 28th June 1926 and shows the intimacy and the tone of complicity between the two. The second one, addressed to his aunt Teresa Piccolo and dated 16th October 1938, quite different in style and content, expresses the family's anxieties over his mother's health. The final item in the Appendix is a double postcard-letter written by Lampedusa's future wife Alessandra Wolff (Licy) before 1929.

The letters to the Piccolos are composed in the same sparkling style as their conversations during the many meetings between the cousins in which I had the good fortune to participate. This style is the precursor of the language of *The Leopard* and the short stories, and also of that particular, original way of perceiving the external world which played such a great part in the author's success. His unerring, introspective, mordant eye on the human comedy is all here already – a feature which is no small thing in the narrator's characterization.

These letters describe the typical summer itinerary of Lampedusa in the Twenties: a long journey through Europe, beginning with a prolonged stay in England and followed by a brief tour of France and a flying visit to Austria, before joining his mother for a stay in the Tyrol. For 1927 we have a summer's correspondence (eighteen letters) which we may regard as almost complete. From 1928 we are left with only six letters, which repeat a similar itinerary (before reaching Innsbruck, Lampedusa passes through Zurich). In 1929 we have two letters from Rome, and in 1930 three from Berlin which refer to a journey to the Baltic: this is when the relationship which would lead to the writer's marriage began. One letter, quite a different one, goes back to 1925 and is the most "Italian" of the collection.

The discovery of these letters enriches, without the need for any substantial revision of it, my own acquaintance with Tomasi di Lampedusa and the three Piccolo siblings, Agata Giovanna (1891–1974), Casimiro (1894–1970) and Lucio (1901–69). Some conclusions that I had deduced from my many visits to Capo d'Orlando and from the tales of Lampedusa about his cousins in the years '53–57 have been confirmed, in particular regarding the special role which each of the brothers played within the family circle, and also their relation to the outside world. When in 1953 I went for the first time to Capo d'Orlando, Baronessa Teresa, the mother of the three siblings, was gravely ill. She was to die in December of that year. From 1954 I often went to Capo d'Orlando, as a guest of the Piccolos. The visits gradually became more frequent, and in 1956–57 they were fortnightly and lasted for two or three days.

The Piccolos seemed to live in a magical world made up of cultural and personal allusions, a continual game of nods and winks in which both Casimiro and Lucio excelled. Having climbed the short flight of steps up to their villa, one reached a vast anteroom. This, and a broad corridor, divided the villa into two. On the right there were two rooms for guests and the dining room. On the left the siblings' bedrooms, which I never entered except to visit Giovanna when she was failing. In the last years of her life she lived under judicial seals set up everywhere as a result of the dispute which Lucio's son, Giuseppe, had initiated with his aunt and uncles and with the Fondazione Famiglia Piccolo di Calanovella founded by them. Even Lampedusa told me that he had been in there only on one occasion, when his Aunt Teresa had died, while my wife Mirella had entered a couple of times with Giovanna, perhaps because of a strong feeling of female solidarity.

At the end of the corridor was the large drawing room looking out onto the sea. It was furnished in a strange way, with that casual appearance which marked the style of the house and was particularly evident in this room and in the dining room next to it. Here there were various objects piled up over months and years: magazines on spiritualism and on gardening, and various bits of kitsch given as presents by the servants, were lying on the shelves and on some small armchairs, making the right-hand side of the room – where, in addition, Lucio Piccolo's upright piano stood – totally unusable. On the left-hand side was Casimiro's armchair with, in front of it, what was for the time a huge television. This was an enclosed area. Casimiro had an obsessive-compulsive disorder and needed his own separate, uncontaminated space. His hands often looked reddened and chapped by their frequent disinfection with alcohol. In front, on the terrace with its view of the sea, were placed two small settees at right angles to the central window. They were reserved for Giovanna and for guests. In this room poetry was not spoken of, or rather this was not Lucio's domain, and the chief character here was by turns Giovanna or Casimiro. Both of them had read widely. Giovanna, who was confined to a domestic role, talked mainly about female skills and gardening. But Casimiro was an inexhaustible mine of pleasant literary reminiscences. He was the dominant figure in the room, whether he was speaking about literature (he was fully acquainted with French literature of the end of the century, particularly Anatole France) or about spiritualism, photography or painting, which he could judge as a professional. His art criticism was not indeed stylistic, but he could distinguish instances of toning-down, focal points and, especially, skill in the brushwork. It was precisely for this last characteristic that the paintings of Velázquez and Goya were for him the pinnacle of that art.

In the drawing room Lucio huddled up in an armchair and was treated as the child of the family, taking no part in serious discussions, whether of administration, politics or social relations. He became part of the conversation only when this moved off – as in fact happened continually – onto visionary matters, and then he could expand and become involved, protected under the cloak of allegories – allegories which usually gave his neighbours a good hiding.

Lucio's domain was rather the entrance hall. The literary guests, who were not taken on to Casimiro's domain, stopped here. Or else, because of the great familiarity and esteem which Lucio had for "the Monster", the entertainment was removed to the bedroom at the front of the house, where the beloved cousin was accommodated. It was there that Lucio dictated and read to us his poetical work as it was created, and where several manuscript versions of his lyrics were written out now by Lampedusa and now by me. Lucio's domain was also reserved for tall stories, with characters from everyday life inserted into a series of fables, where they played the roles of ridiculous heroes. Every character appeared in an imaginary role under a special name: Lampedusa was "the Monster", I was the "Meddling Youth", Pietro Emanuele Sgadari di Lo Monaco was "the Magician" or "the Vizier", Raniero Alliata di Pietratagliata was again "the Magician", Francesco Agnello was "the Bishop", Francesco Orlando was "the Poet", Filippo Cianciafara was "the King", Lucio Papa D'Amico was "Sir Imbroglio", etc. These nicknames, as in the Commedia dell'Arte, predetermined the character's behaviour within the performance.

If I compare these memories with the letters, everything falls into place. Here too the characters have various nicknames, at times more than one for a particular character, and their roles are assigned to them according to the hierarchies from the Fifties. Casimiro is in fact the interlocutor of choice. Despite the fact that only four letters are expressly addressed to him, and two to Lucio, while the rest are for both of them, the main interlocutor always remains Casimiro, and it can be inferred that he is also predominantly the author of the replies.

A recurrent feature, in the letters as much as in the conversations, was the constant banter about sexual practices – quite singular today, but in accordance with social customs in my youth, that is to say between 1940 and 1960. That last date can also be taken as the *terminus a quo* of the general collapse of agrarian revenues in Sicilian society. If that society had already been creaking for some time, by the end of the Fifties it had dissolved into the Lampedusian "flight of swallows". The sexual chit-chat reflected in fact the habits of a certain social class absorbed in *otia*, not very sensitive, unmindful of what was happening in the wide world. For our characters, the place of choice for this *otia* was the Bellini Club, haunt of the aristocrats and their charmed lives.

In this regard, the Lampedusa of the middle of the Twenties was quite different from the Lampedusa of the Fifties. The Villa della Piana continued to radiate the childish enchantment of Santa Margherita and of times past, and he adored it for this reason. But he had had a hard life – in the aftermath of the Second World War a very hard one – and all the time he directed his antennae towards the external world, intent on helping the Sicilians of the new generation to avoid the isolation and the consequent behaviour that had afflicted his generation. Only at the Piana was everything as it used to be. The "Monster" knew that, and he recorded his observation in an expression of affectionate melancholy: "The Piccolos not only believe in the continuance of contact with the dead, but they assume, even after their death, the everlasting survival of the Piana, where their mother, the three of them, and their dogs will continue to hang about among the citrus groves, buzzards and agapanthi – and, *last but not least*, their foremen, peasants and domestics will still provide service".

As the letters published here reveal, Lampedusa's opinions as a traveller evolved over the years from 1925 to 1930. He had travelled on his own through London, England, Paris, in a sort of survey of scenes from literature, while always keeping in mind the consolations of being alone. He mentions with affection the total solitude of metropolises as described by Rilke in his *Aufzeichnungen des Malte Laurids Brigge*. But when he reaches Berlin in 1930 and witnesses various depravities in the *cafés chantants*, the sinister atmosphere hanging over Germany is revealed to his traveller's eyes. The Germans "within ten years will, I think, send every nation a note, by means of the waiter..." This eccentric prince was far-sighted: the time of *otia*, of sexual gossip is slipping through the fingers. Within ten years, if not before, the trumpets of the Apocalypse will sound.

LETTERS FROM LONDON
AND EUROPE

1925

I

Dear Casimiro,

I'm very excited about the latest political events. A few days ago, the attack on Amendola filled me with exquisite pleasure, and now the sight of Palermo under the spotlight in Italian, even European politics makes me really proud.* I should like to hope that you will win and show that Palermo, although it has no facilities for cleaning the streets, is not without the facility for a political clean sweep. The imminent duel (or rather tournament) between the Prefect and Trabia, Cesarò and Arenella* will be a very interesting spectacle, and a profoundly comic one – and if I were a millionaire I should not hesitate for an instant before returning to Palermo just to be there while it is taking place.

And the Bellini!* Oh, the Bellini, the blood of whose Swordsman is at this moment in danger of coursing through the eminently Bellinian enterprise of the Aventine Secession!*

"*J'ai vu mourir Louis XVI et Bonaparte*"* – or, if not that, I have in my lifetime seen more than one memorable action. I have seen Raniero the Magician play mah-jong,* I have seen the swans which cleave the velvety waters of the Lake of Love in Bruges; I have seen Piccadilly at midday

5

and Montmartre at midnight; I have seen Michelangelo's Moses and I have heard Masnata talk about antiquity;* I have breakfasted more than once with Pirandello and I have conversed with Raimondo Arenella; I have seen the beauty of the Princess Yolanda and the ugliness of her husband;* I have walked beneath the centuries-old limes in Windsor and beneath the famous cypresses in Fiesole; I have seen war and the crueller aftermath of war; I have seen Mussolini in his black shirt and young Alice in court dress;* I have eaten "*cailles truffées au champagne*" with Lady Vanderbilt and I have starved on the millet of *Kriegsgefangen*;* I have seen the Turners in the Tate Gallery, the Memlings in Bruges and the Raphaels in the Louvre; I know Dante, I love Shakespeare, I have read Goethe and have endured the poems of Lucio;* I have seen the eyes of Rosalind and the legs of Mary Ashley;* I am acquainted with the peaceful dignity of Vicenza and the vulgarity of Brussels; I have endured every kind of fate: the Viceroy of India has insisted that I should go before him through a door; I have been mocked by Corradino; in Modena I have paid court to the daughter of an innkeeper and in London to Lady Beauchamps;* I have been in all sorts of situations and been equal to them all. I repeat: "*J'ai vu mourir Louis XIV et Bonaparte.*"

And yet I would give up all these experiences, I would wipe them all out of my memory, to have the pleasure of being present for one hour these days at a session of the Bellini.

At Antwerp, in the famous zoological garden, I have seen *le palais des singes* – in an immense cage, more than three hundred monkeys with every kind of phizog and every colour of buttock were giving themselves over to obscene frolicking and quick-witted pursuits, and were trying, in vain, to make us blush for our ancestors. All the same I am confident that that cage is a model of the highest spirituality, of dignified composure, of calm beauty, a kind of garden of Academe or salon of Madame Rambouillet, in comparison with the Bellini these days.*

Lucky you who can at this stage store up enough amusement to provide all you will need during a long life.

* * *

Together with this letter I am sending you a pamphlet on the exhibition of Decorative Arts which is taking place here. It is extremely interesting: the examples of architecture are magnificent, and the furniture and the interior decorations are in no way inferior. I have the impression that at long last a twentieth-century style has been found. It would interest you enormously. And then the display is magnificent, especially in the evening. The Austrian and Czech pavilions are the best. The Italian pavilion, which is interesting enough on the inside, is on the outside, in utter incomprehension of the object of the exhibition, in the Renaissance style with the added annoyance of an interminable Latin inscription. But the public is always philistine: from what I hear it is one of those which are most successful with the crowd. It is also sad to observe the total incomprehension and the cheap mockery by the public of all the other beautiful things, and since there is here no question of fine art but of buildings to construct, furniture to sell and decorations to market, the bourgeois taste of the public is a serious matter and could result in the failure of this artistic impulse.

* * *

In a bookshop on the Rue Royale a whole window is devoted to books on Fascism and portraits of Mussolini at all stages of his life, in various poses and costumes. Incidentally, in the newspapers here, disquieting rumours have recently been circulating about his death. What do they say about it where you are?*

In one of the side roads there is a kind of fair, and among other things there is a game of "roulette", in which instead of numbers there are the flags of the various nations. I watched it for a little while, and the ball stopped at the Italian flag, and the man announced: "*C'est l'Italie qui a gagné.*" And a young man in the crowd said to his friend: "*Je te crois; avec leur Mussolini!*"*

Small symptoms.

Here, on the other hand, I am in a potentially Bolshevist country. The situation is very serious. But, just notice how important national honour is: I don't give a damn, because I know that even if a revolution breaks out, no one will touch a hair on my head or steal one penny from me, because by my side I have… Mussolini!

That's enough: I must go out now.

I repeat my encouragement and my good wishes for the battle of 2nd August. Which I will follow step by step in the *Giornale di Sicilia* which reaches even up here.

Please remember me to Aunt and Giovanna,* and even to Lucio, who I hope will reply to my polite letter from Brussels.

Affectionate regards

The French Monster

I include a postcard of a delightful Egyptian statuette in the Louvre.

NOTES

Two numbered sheets, each one folded in order to give four pages. On the top left corner of the first page, inside a box drawn in ink: "Giuseppe Tomasi / Hôtel Vouillemont / 15 – rue Boissy-d'Anglas".

p. 5, *the attack on Amendola… makes me proud*: The Deputy Giovanni Amendola had been attacked by the Fascists at Montecatini on 21st July. He did not recover, and he was to die in a clinic in Cannes in April 1926. Amendola had been an interventionist, but after the War he became connected with Francesco Saverio Nitti's party, which advocated the development and industrialization of southern Italy. In 1922 he had founded the anti-Fascist party Unione Democratica Nazionale, which was most active in the South of Italy. Hospitalized after the attack, he was visited by various parliamentarians. Even the Prince of Trabia, a senator of the Kingdom, went to visit him. In Palermo the campaign for the local elections was underway. In the *Giornale di Sicilia* for 22nd–23rd July 1925, Lampedusa had read: "Sicily has become fashionable for the last four or five days".

p. 5, *Trabia, Cesarò and Arenella*: Pietro Lanza Branciforte, Prince of Trabia, saw his supremacy over the Palermitan aristocracy recognized. He was nicknamed "the Viceroy". Giovanni Antonio Colonna, Duke of Cesarò, was an MP for several terms, and Minister for Post and Telegraphy from 1922 to 1924. Giuseppe Valguarnera, Duke of Arenella and Prince of Niscemi, was the nephew of Corrado Valguarnera di Niscemi. A *garibaldino* and the model for Tancredi Falconeri in *The Leopard*, he was Giuseppe Tomasi di Lampedusa's cousin.

p. 5, *the Bellini*: An aristocratic club founded in Palermo in 1769 as the Grand Salon of the Nobility. In 1864 it was named The Bellini Club. It was situated next to the Bellini Theatre, known before 1860 as the Caroline Theatre. Many of Lampedusa's allusions to the Piccolos originate in conversations and remarks in the Bellini Club. Most noticeably present in the letters are many members who joined in the years 1919–25. They are: Fulco Santostefano della Cerda, Duke of Verdura (1919); Raniero Alliata di Pietratagliata (1921); Corrado Valguarnera, Prince of Niscemi (1921); Francesco Notarbartolo, Prince of Sciara and Castelreale (1921); Pietro Notarbartolo of Salandra (1921); Giuseppe Tomasi, Duke of Palma: the writer, with the title he bore before the death of his father (1922); Corrado Parodi Giusino di Belsito (1922); Fortunio Parodi Giusino di Belsito (1922); Casimiro Piccolo di Calanovella (1923); Lucio Piccolo di Calanovella (1923); Pietro Papè di Pratameno (1923); Pietro Emanuele Sgadari di Lo Monaco (1923); Corrado Fatta (1925); Gutierrez Spadafora, Prince of Spadafora (1925).

p. 5, *Swordsman... Aventine Secession*: The Aventine Secession, named after the episode in 494 BC Rome, was the withdrawal of the Italian Socialist Party from Parliament as a protest following the murder of Giacomo Matteotti.

p. 5, *J'ai vu mourir Louis XVI et Bonaparte*: "I have seen the deaths of Louis XVI and Bonaparte." The quotation is from Chateaubriand's Note to his *Life of Rancé*. It continues: "What is point of going on living after that? What am I doing in the world?"

p. 5, *Raniero the Magician play mah-jong*: A reference to the entomologist Raniero Alliata di Pietratagliata, Prince of the Holy Roman Empire (see also note to p. 15). In the slang of the letters, the word mah-jong is also used as a nickname in Letters II, III, V and as a euphemism for "testicles" in Letter XVII.

p. 6, *Masnata talk about antiquity*: In the letters, Masnata is mocked as a dilettante antiquarian involved in a homosexual affair. He is not one of the members of the Bellini Club, at that time exclusively aristocratic. A possible identification among the upper middle class of Palermo would be with the lawyer Giovanni Masnata, who lived at No. 2 Via Gaetano Daita.

p. 6, *Pirandello... Raimondo Arenella... Princess Yolanda and... her husband*: Lampedusa came to know Pirandello at the Italian Embassy, where the Marquess della Torretta and his secretary Ugo Sola gave a small reception. Raimondo Arenella was the younger son of Giuseppe Valguarnera, Duke of Arenella. Princess Yolanda of Savoy, was the firstborn of Victor Emmanuel III and wife of Giorgio Carlo Calvi, Count Bergolo.

p. 6, *young Alice in court dress*: A reference to Alice Barbi, wife of Pietro Tomasi della Torretta, Giuseppe Tomasi di Lampedusa's uncle. She was a celebrated Lieder singer and a muse to Johannes Brahms in his old age. In the family she was known by the nickname of "young Alice", because she was fifteen years older than her husband: she was born in Modena in 1858, while Pietro Tomasi was born in Palermo in 1873.

p. 6, *Lady Vanderbilt... Kriegsgefangen*: Lady Vanderbilt was Alva Erskine Smith, the wife of William Kissan Vanderbilt. The Vanderbilt family owned the most important railways in the United States. William and Alva were the parents of Consuelo Vanderbilt, wife of the Duke of Marlborough. *Kriegsgefangener* (misspelt in the manuscript): "prisoner of war" (German).

p. 6, *and have endured the poems of Lucio*: A reference to Lucio Piccolo di Calanovella, first cousin of Giuseppe Tomasi di Lampedusa, composer and poet, younger brother of Casimiro and Giovanna. He was discovered in 1954 by Eugenio Montale, who wrote the foreword to *Canti barocchi e altre liriche* (Milan: Mondadori, 1956). His poetical works have been translated into English: *Collected Poems of Lucio Piccolo*, translated by Brian Swan and Ruth Feldman (Princeton, NJ: Princeton University Press, 1972).

p. 6, *Rosalind... Mary Ashley*: Rosalind is a character in Shakespeare's *As You Like It*. As to "Mary Ashley", the most likely hypothesis is that the author is referring to Sylvia Hawkes, a famous beauty in international high society who married Lord Ashley, from whom she divorced in 1935. Lady Ashley

11

married successively Douglas Fairbanks Jr., Lord Stanley of Alderley, Clark Gable and Prince Dimitri Djordjadze. Tomasi calls her Mary, and this does not tally with the identification, but in the photographs from the Twenties Lady Ashley's legs were truly amazing.

p. 6, *Corradino... Lady Beauchamps*: Corradino Parodi Giusino di Belsito, cousin of the Valguarneras and the Tomasis, was reputed to have a poisonous tongue. The Beauchamps, an English family of Norman origin, had been the ancient owners of Warwick Castle, the most renowned medieval castle in England. The castle and the title passed to the Grevilles. It is hard to say who this Lady Beauchamps in the early Twenties could be.

p. 7, *garden of Academe... the Bellini these days*: The garden of Academe was a sacred grove on the outskirts of Athens surrounding the tomb of the Attic hero Academus. It was in this grove that Plato set up his school, the Academy. The "salon of Madame Rambouillet" is a reference to the sixteenth-century Parisian salon "of good taste and propriety" of Catherine de Vivonne, Marquise de Rambouillet.

p. 8, *disquieting rumours... where you are*: Mussolini, who was suffering from a fit of gastric ulcer, was rumoured to be dying in that period.

p. 8, *C'est l'Italie qui a gagné... Je te crois; avec leur Mussolini*: "It's Italy who's won... Of course, with their Mussolini!" (French).

p. 8, *Aunt and Giovanna*: A reference to Teresa Piccolo, mother of the three Piccolo siblings and maternal aunt of Lampedusa, and Giovanna Piccolo di Calanovella, sister of Casimiro and Lucio.

1926 and 1927

The pictures in the following
plate section are from Lampedusa's
photo albums of his journey
to England in 1926

Giuseppe Tomasi di Lampedusa at the
Italian Embassy in London in 1926.

The Italian Embassy in
Grosvenor Square.

Hertford House, which holds
the Wallace Collection.

A drawing room in the Italian Embassy.

The "more than human London *policeman*".

Bond Street "at 11 a.m."

Regent Street.

Piccadilly Circus
"from the double-decker bus".

A view of the Thames from
London Bridge.

Giuseppe Tomasi di Lampedusa
in St James's Park.

Alice Barbi on "The Ladies' Mile"
in Hyde Park.

A view of Whitehall from St James's Park.

The Orangery in Kensington Park.

Holland Park gardens.

Hampton Court gardens.

Hampton Court Palace.

The Bridge House Hotel in Staines.

II

The image is no doubt stale: I myself, unless I am mistaken, have used it already. I am however forced to make use of it again, because it is accurate: thinking of Palermo from here one sees a large town, low-lying and red-hot, enclosed in a circle of steel-grey cliffs, the whole enveloped in a great cloud of reddish dust. I know, I do, that within this cloud noble hearts and exquisite artists swirl about, poets and painters like those to whom I have the honour to write, expert embroiderers like Fortunello, profound antiquaries like Masnata, distillers of exquisite essences like Mah-Jong, rivals of Bacon in natural philosophy like O.S., critics like Bebbuzzo, beautiful ladies like Carolina Salandra, ephebes like Planeta, learned humanists like Pitruzzo, a gathering of magnanimous spirits who would honour any Athens – all secretly guided by the supreme Areopagus which sits within the I-don't-know-whether-ruined-or-never-finished walls of Palazzo Villarosa.*

I know about these things: I am honoured by the friendship which many of these sages accord me: it is my proudest boast to take part (even if without a deliberative vote) in the august assembly which meets in that ornate Acropolis.

But the impression remains.

15

* * *

Imagine a cat, a common *felis catus*, moving about inside the great cages of the zoological garden. He knows that those tigers "burning bright",* those regal lions, the panthers and the leopards are his close relatives; he notes the same curling of the tail in the tiger which he has so often examined in the mirror; he sees how the lion bites and chews the haunch of horse in the same way as he himself handles a chicken wing. Even so, in the presence of such super-cats, his wretched fur bristles on his feeble back, and these brothers and cousins are too powerfully developed for him to recognize in them his own flesh and blood.

So it is with a Bellinian (the Monster) when he is shown in among these giants of Bellinianism who assemble in the clubs here.

Postulate: a Bellinian is in relation to the English Bellinians as your cat is to your genuine tiger.

An edifice (or rather, first a street – Pall Mall – all massive clubs, indestructible, secret; few vehicles – the local Bellinians have so arranged it that the omnibuses do not profane it with their menial wheels – few shops and all of them men's shops: shotguns at a hundred pounds each; fishing rods and harpoons for whaling; various liquors; cigars ten shillings each. Policemen who watch over the cars of the honourable members. The smell of petrol, of tar and of Havanas – the silence of a sacred wood).

An edifice. Privately owned, above all: hence the absence of a landlord, of the fear of an increase in the rent, of the terror of eviction – the certainty of being able to Bellinize on the same armchair for century after century.

Five floors. Bellinian style: a compromise between baroque and neoclassic; Portland stone which absorbs smuts and transforms them into amber. Six or seven steps rising from the street, low and broad, a symbol of hospitality; a door which is both high and narrow, to signify at the same time the difficulty in gaining admission and its importance. Entrance hall: grey marble; at the end, a bronze statue of Lord Beaconsfield, patron god, sarcastic and malicious (it was he who called them "magnificent asses", but since they are Bellinians they don't realize it).* Ten manservants, each 1.90 metres tall: blue livery, chamois leather boots – everything *clean*. On the right a colossal engine of war in mahogany containing a super-servant, a "*carrier*" for correspondence and other things; on the left a door leading to the waiting rooms for non-members.

Further back still, "toilets": a public urinal in black marble, covered on the inside in porcelain: 20 places. Washbowls with water hot enough to take the skin off your hands, and nail brushes such as exist nowhere else. In the back, a washroom to provide the finishing touches. On the left, a wardrobe.

Hall: colossal, round, with a dome – a host of leather armchairs (genuine and gleaming) and sofas, writing desks with silver inkwells as big as the bier of a newborn child, paper-holders of Babylonian bulk. Various Bellinians talking with each other: clothed in very heavy material of fantastic cut, coloured shirts with stiff collars *idem*. Now it is time to formulate a fundamental theorem:

The London Bellinian, unlike the Palermitan subspecies, is always perfectly washed and clean-shaven. Old generals in retirement, rosy and snowy, wearing spats; lean lords with large noses and red carnations in their buttonholes; Members of Parliament who chew at their cigars and spit in the heat of discussion.

Reading room. Oak-panelled, ceiling of white plaster-work. Portraits in oil of illustrious members – above the red-marble fireplace a Reynolds. Library: huge – 10,000 volumes, a magnificent cabinet-maker's piece, eighteenth-century, brought over from the club's old building – walnut with a little gilding – ceiling by Hofner* depicting Knowledge descending among the Bellinians. Two big ancient maps of the world at the back. A Chippendale table in the middle with atlases and other little things. Everything three times life-size.

On the right a string of reception rooms on a more human scale: little smoking rooms for special conversations, three or four halls with lovely bright antique hangings – in one of them a collection of the club's oriental porcelain (the bequest of a deceased member) – games rooms.

On the first floor: a *restaurant* – three bright rooms with small tables, very fine linen, many flowers, silverware to lift the spirits. In another wing an innumerable series of little rooms for the members, where they always keep a tailcoat and other garments to change into without going home.

Bedrooms above.

Excellent cuisine (French, fortunately). The London Bellinian despises the *caciotti** and boiled pumpkin, which are the staple food of the Palermitan species. And the table d'hôte consists of lobster, sumptuous meat *pies* and strawberries (this is *lunch*, you understand).

Boundless kindness: the Monster realizes that he is an eminent personage – he is seated between Shaftesbury, his host, and the Duke of Marlborough,* opposite a lord whose name he does not know but whom he addresses *de confiance* as "Mylord". He expresses himself in an English which is flowery and vaguely Elizabethan; he is pleased that he had a "manicure" two days ago, but when he looks at the clothes of his fellow diners and compares them with his own, he cannot understand why Bevilacqua* does not work instead as a blacksmith, for which he may well have a real bent.

When the table was cleared, he smoked a certain number of excellent cigarettes, whose make he does not know because they bore only the monogram of the club, offered his thanks and left. He does however have an invitation to frequent the sacred places, where he will have the advantage of eating well at a modest price, without the trouble of introductions, which sensibly have been dispensed with.

* * *

Later the Monster will give a detailed account of his dealings with His Highness the Rajah of Baroda, with particular reference to the Rani, something which will please Casimiro the Indianologist.* It cannot be denied that this queen is a truly remarkable creature, and worthy of unremitting admiration. He reaffirms however his own exclusive cult of the West, and observes that the beauty of that Hindu is perfect precisely because she looks like an Italian beauty.

He finishes here, and with best wishes he signs himself

The Monster of Mayfair

This letter was written over several days; the Monster is now at the Great Central Hôtel, Marylebone Road, London N.W.*

NOTES

On paper with the heading of the hotel where Lampedusa was staying: "Hotel Curzon, Curzon Street, Mayfair, London. W." Four numbered sheets (eight sides) of light-blue paper. The date is written slantwise on the left.

p. 15, *thinking of Palermo… Palazzo Villarosa*: The description of Palermo is in the language of Dante's *Inferno*. The Bellini Club is a parody of the "noble castle" which, in the *Inferno* (Canto IV), encloses the "great spirits". In the Palermitan "great cloud of reddish dust", the members of the Bellini are swirling as the crowd of the pusillanimous damned are "always swirling / Throughout that unrelieved black atmosphere" (III, 28–29). See also second note to p. 88. "Fortunello" is a reference to Fortunio Parodi Giusino di Belsito, called an "embroiderer" because of his eloquent gossiping. He is the elder brother of Corrado (Corradino): see seventh note to p. 6. For Masnata, see first note to p. 6. From this passage, he would appear to be a member of the Bellini, but he is not on the list of members for that year. Therefore Masnata and Mah-Jong, although immersed in the great cloud of reddish dust, were probably not members of the supreme Areopagus. From the other passages where he is mentioned, Mah-Jong would appear to be one of the Piccolos' servants. His characteristics are being unwashed and looking like a monkey (see also sixth note to p. 5). O.S. stands for "Old Swine" and is a reference to the entomologist Raniero Alliata di Pietratagliata (see sixth note to p. 5), also alluded to as a "Magician" because of his esoteric and spiritualist interests. He was a skilful maker of lead soldiers: his friends collected used toothpaste tubes to provide him with the material. "Bebbuzzo" is Pietro Emanuele Sgadari di Lo Monaco, a musical critic for the *Giornale di Sicilia*. In the Thirties he translated Ronsard and Villon, and was the author of a list of Sicilian painters. He too was occasionally nicknamed the "Magician". Carolina Notarbartolo di Salandra, whose beauty is put into question by Lampedusa, was the wife of Pietro Notarbartolo, a member of the Bellini Club. Santi Planeta, who was renowned for his ugliness, became a member of the Bellini only in 1934. "Pitruzzo" is a reference to Pietro Papè, Duke of Pratameno. The Palazzo Notarbartolo di Villarosa occupied the whole extent of Via Ruggero Settimo – one of the main streets in Palermo – between Via Generale Magliocco and Piazza Regalmici (the so-called "Quattro Campi di Campagna"). The building's construction was interrupted on the first floor. The Bellini Club had its rooms in the Palace, on the side of Piazza Regalmici.

p. 16, *tigers "burning bright"*: From William Blake's poem 'The Tyger', from his *Songs of Experience*. The quotation is in English in the manuscript.

p. 17, *Lord Beaconsfield… they don't realize it*: A reference to Benjamin Disraeli, Earl of Beaconsfield.

p. 18, *Hofner*: Probably a reference to the landscape artist and animal painter Johann Baptist Hofner (1832–1913).

p. 18, *caciotti*: The *caciottu* is a small focaccia filled with lard, cheese, and fresh ricotta (Sicilian).

p. 18, *Shaftesbury… the Duke of Marlborough*: A reference to Anthony Ashley, Earl of Shaftesbury, and Charles Spencer Churchill, Duke of Marlborough and first cousin of Sir Winston Churchill.

p. 19, *Bevilacqua*: A very prestigious men's tailor's in Palermo.

p. 19, *Casimiro the Indianologist*: Casimiro Piccolo favoured fairy and oriental subjects for his watercolours. He emulated the illustrations in English books, particularly those in Kipling's (hence the appellation "Indianologist"). A rani is the wife of a rajah.

p. 19, *This letter was written… London N.W.*: This note was added above the heading of the hotel.

III

London, 5th July '27

The Monster is sending a second instalment. It would be superfluous to describe again the clothes, customs and the panther of the Rajah, because this has been done already, and he has requested that word should be sent to the professional Indianologist,* who is a professional in those descriptions. He will add only that the panther is called (*of course*) Bagheera,* in an amazing repercussion on the East of Western art which has in its turn been orientalized, and that Her Highness the Rani (who is in her own right the Lady of Lahore) has been, when she was a child – which was only a short time ago – to Palermo and has told me that the mountains of the Conca d'Oro* bear an extraordinary resemblance to those in Nepal, which will please the Indianologist: standing now on the balcony – with Lucio naked and turbaned acting as a fakir after thirty years of fasting on a bed of nails, and Mah-Jong* in a plane tree in the role of a big monkey – he will be able to fancy that he finds himself in the land of his dreams.

The Monster's land of dreams is, on the contrary, this. "*Luxe, calme et volupté.*"* This city is perhaps the only one that can evoke the same emotions as nature – indeed it isn't a city, but a wood in which, together with the most dismal trees, houses have grown too. Nothing artificial, no building plan: everything happening spontaneously, governed only by an inner rhythm. A silent activity, order without coercion, the greatest agglomeration of human beings – and at every step the feeling of the countryside, pale-skinned women, men wearing clothes with great pleats in them, shops which sell, for an appropriate number of pounds, Chinese jade, enamels from Limoges and walking sticks by Brigg, a bookshop (a recent discovery by the Monster) where there is *everything*, *restaurants* where you can eat pasta with sardines, bird's nest soup and *mulligatawny* (Indianologist!). You can see marbles by Phidias and Buddhist terracottas, Persian miniatures and Italian and German incunabula, 672 people run over and killed by motor cars in six months, shoes walking from dawn to midnight without a speck of dust on them, 4 million lire taken in one day in a collection for the hospitals, and the *policeman* – that very *policeman* who on the Day of Judgement will certainly be chosen to allow past, with a gesture of the hand, on the right the elect with the Monster at their head, and on the left the reprobates led by the Spectral Tarsier.*

Poker. Several evenings ago. After dining with Londonderry. The Monster sunk in an armchair, smoking and contemplating a Corot. The master of the house arrives, with the ribbon of the Garter on his paunch:* "*Do you play poker, my dear Duke?*" The Monster takes refuge in serpentine caution: "*So sorry, Mylord, I have never been able to learn.*" A little later he approaches the table, sits down and observes. He sees mother-of-pearl tokens changing hands, bets being raised enormously, and he asks timidly how much is the initial bet. "Only ten pounds, it's a family game." Around 900 lire.*

The Monster retires, goes back to contemplating the Corot, meditates on the theory of increasing poverty. "We are poor, we shall die poor."*

* * *

Intermezzo – *The Daily Telegraph*. Classical performances from Ostia, Pompeii and Syracuse. Talk of "Maestro Josephus Mulè". Are you not pleased by such humanism grafted onto a trunk from Termini?*

* * *

The Monster is tired now. He must get dressed shortly to go and lunch at the Embassy – where he is always received, it must be said, with the greatest honour, and escorted out by His Excellency himself up to the front door. The Monster believes that this morning he went too far at breakfast, and that 4 rolls, 4 rounds of *toast* (they don't exist anywhere else), a slice of *cake*, then butter and apricot jam, then 2 cups of coffee with milk are too much for his delicate stomach. The Monster is therefore stopping writing.

He wishes however to notify those gentlemen, Casimiro and Lucio, that if one day (which he hopes will be soon) they decide to visit these shores, it is quite pointless to do so without the Monster, because by themselves they will certainly see Westminster, the Tower of London and the museums, but they will understand nothing at all of the city and its soul without the Monster, who holds the keys to it.

The *over-fed* Monster.

NOTES

On paper headed "Hôtel Great Central, London, N.W. 1". Two sheets, four sides.

p. 23, *the professional Indianologist*: See second note to p. 19.

p. 23, *Bagheera*: The name of the black panther in Rudyard Kipling's *The Jungle Book*.

p. 23, *Conca d'Oro*: The Conca d'Oro – situated between the Mounts of Palermo and the Tyrrhenian Sea – is the plain surrounding the city.

p. 23, *Mah-Jong*: See note to p. 15.

p. 23, *Luxe, calme et volupté*: The quote is from Charles Baudelaire's poem 'Invitation to the Voyage', from *The Flowers of Evil*.

p. 24, *the Spectral Tarsier*: The "Spectral Tarsier" is probably a reference to Lucio Piccolo, although it could also be directed to the monkey-like Mah-Jong mentioned above.

p. 24, *Londonderry... paunch*: Charles Vane-Tempest-Stewart, 7th Marquess Londonderry. He had been made Knight of the Garter in 1919.

p. 24, *ten pounds... around 900 lire*: Over five hundred pounds in today's money.

p. 25, *We are poor, we shall die poor*: The tone is the same as that of Don Fabrizio in *The Leopard*: "We are old, Chevalley, very old". The same expression is used in Letter IX.

p. 25, *Maestro Josephus Mulè... Termini*: Giuseppe Mulè was a Sicilian composer from Termini Imerese. He was the author of a variety of theatrical music for the classical performances in Syracuse when Ettore Romagnoli was the director.

IV

The Monster continues his pilgrimage through *old England*. An itinerary devised by himself, with his usual acumen, takes him through the most ancient cities of this glorious island. He has carefully avoided the big cities, the industrial infernos of Manchester, Birmingham, Liverpool and Sheffield, and kept above all to the venerable cathedral cities, to the peaceful seats of learning. The rambling Monster has tried everything these last few days. In Cambridge he put up at the Red Lion, which was doubtless the model which inspired Dickens with the nocturnal blunders of the great Pickwick through the maze-like intricacies of a corridor.* The following day, at Lincoln, he found himself in a *family hotel*, one of those severe and dignified institutions which jealously preserve the moral patrimony of the Victorian era – all in all gracious, if stylized to the extreme, with an excellent cuisine in a dining room out of the pages of Meredith or Jane Austen. And since yesterday he has been in a vast hotel, overlooking a large garden where, for an incredibly reasonable price, he is occupying a sumptuous room and being served with refined and rare dishes.

But these are secondary elements: for three days he has travelled through the amazing serenity of the English countryside: meadows with herds of cattle, lazy brimful rivers, gorgeous hills – a real pastoral scene from Sir Philip Sidney.* And what cities! In what moment of aberration did the Monster say that artistic beauty was a secondary matter in England? A hasty judgement by a normally cautious spirit, who can plead as his excuse only his ignorance of the true England and an error caused by a cosmopolis such as London.

Cambridge, with its fourteenth-century colleges, enclosed secular cloisters, a well-endowed seat of uninterrupted learning; Ely, tragic, impoverished, the birthplace of the proud mother of the great Oliver,* with its boundless landscape of wretched marshes beneath a leaden sky, where the divine cathedral stands on its rock, austere and yet maternal offspring of the faith of the Middle Ages, raising a prayer which could not but be well received. Never, declares the Monster, did he experience a more intense artistic emotion, because he has never come across a landscape and a work of art corresponding more intimately to each other, and he has never been swept more promptly into that glorious twelfth century which was the golden age of Christian civilization in the world.

A great race those Normans! And I wish the Lord had kept us for several centuries under their energetic wisdom! To think that all these incomparable cathedrals were founded on the sites of old Saxon churches, in the first ten years of the Conquest! When we moderns boast of our "zeal for building" we must seem ridiculous to those saints and artists looking down at us from heaven.

And Lincoln! There too the cathedral, built on a very high hill, watches over the industrious city which spreads out at its foot. The lofty, harmonious towers, the incredibly rich decorative detail, the magnificent statues of kings, saints, angels and demons which adorn it make it one of

LETTERS FROM LONDON AND EUROPE • 1927

the most venerable sanctuaries of Christianity. It is needless to sing the praises of York. The capital of Roman Britain, the city of the *pale and angry rose** fulfils and surpasses all the promise of its illustrious name. Here too the cathedral dominates everything, and even at night its enormous mass fills the horizon and makes it holy. But it is in the daytime that it shines, with those windows which are its incomparable glory – intact since the twelfth century, escaping, by a sheer miracle, the iconoclastic fury of Cromwell's soldiers, they continue to make the air enchanted, and every other light that has not passed through their other-worldly colours looks like darkness. The medieval walls of the city – which extend in an uninterrupted circle decorated on top with enormous beds of symbolic white roses in their full pride – are splendid too.

Now the Monster realizes why England, popularly believed to be preoccupied with selling coal and launching battleships, has produced the most sublime poets of European literature. And the Monster, a Roman Catholic and one of the pillars of the Church, weeps at the thought that this country, in which the Christian centuries erected such superlative monuments to its zeal, has escaped from the paternal authority of St Peter's successor; it has besides been punished artistically, because when it was outside the fold, the wonders of Ely, Lincoln and York were superseded by their papier-mâché St Paul's. It must also be noted that the churches are admirably maintained, and that the relative austerity of the Anglican denomination is well suited to the severity of the architecture; and they are free from the deep-blue and red *basinella** too often used by our clergy to adorn the churches, without thinking that much nobler artists than paltry paper hangers have already adorned those walls to the everlasting praise of the Creator.

That is not to deny that the day when a purple cardinal celebrates a Pontifical Mass with incense and hymns on the high altar of Ely or Lincoln will be a truly great event – with or without the red *basinella*.

* * *

But the Monster, as he has already given you to understand, contains in himself not only an angel, but also a pig – of which he is proud. And as a pig he appreciates and rejoices in fleshly pleasures. At times the Spartan simplicity of the pure English cuisine terrifies him. But more often he is delighted – whether he is drinking, as he is today, thick buttery milk which leaves a trace of cream in the cup, whether he is biting bloody *steaks* which pass on to him the vigour of noble and select young bulls, whether he is tasting large thick slices of rosy ham, lying on beds of soft real bread and coming from the heraldic loins of the illustrious hogs of Yorkshire, whether again at the end of the meal, sinking a greedy spoon into the supplies of the lordly cheeses of Chester, rosy as onyx, or Stilton, green as aquamarine, or Cheddar, transparent and amber-coloured. Because here cheese is not served in prosaic slices, but whole cheeses are brought to the table, and the dilettante (I was about to say the lover) digs into the tasty recesses, rummages in them with a horn spoon and tries them out. And the waiters are often so incautious as to leave the multicoloured treasures in front of the Monster – and their eyes pop out when, instead of three cheeses of about ten kilos each, they find only three fragrant but empty shells. "*Bare ruined choirs…*" as the man from Stratford would say.*

Then there are the typists: graceful creatures met on the train or staying in Lincoln at the same hotel as the Monster,

30

who takes them in the evening to the cinema down through the vertical streets of Lindum Colonia. *En tout bien, tout honneur*,* you understand. Anyway, it is more pleasant to have beside you, in the cinema, a typist rather than the poet Lucien de Calenouvelle,* however strikingly feminine his gifts may be, at least according to malicious people, always envious of glory.

Tomorrow evening at 18.30 the Monster will alight at Waverley Station in Edinburgh (pronounced "Eedinboraw"). The said Monster has always had the impression of Scotland – incredibly jagged and thrown down into the middle of the hyperborean seas – as being a sort of slightly milder Iceland. And with its Lammermoors and Lady Macbeths, its witches and its Mary Stuarts, its lochs and its men in skirts, he has always thought of it as Fairyland.

We shall see if that is true. And let us hope that the noble tradition of Scottish hospitality survives, according to which the guest has the right to enjoy not only the home and food of the host but also his wife and daughters. It is true that after the evil done to King Duncan* Scottish hospitality has been under something of a cloud. And the only place where such convenient traditions persist is in fact Palermo (the Iceland of the South), where – at Villa Igiea, Galanti takes hospitable abnegation to the extent of offering the traveller (not indeed his wife) but certainly himself.*

On rereading his letter, the Monster finds that it is badly written but full of a lofty enthusiasm for Gothic churches and for cheeses, for Catholicism and for typists. And enthusiasm is what counts: it saved the sinful Faust, and it will save, we hope,

The Caledonian Monster

* * *

The Monster's address is still Great Central Hôtel, Marylebone Road, London N.W. 1. You must send him a postcard of the Cathedral in Palermo, and write on the back which English cathedral is similar to it.

Whitby or Winchester?*

NOTES

On paper headed "Royal Station Hotel, York". Five numbered sheets, ten sides.

p. 27, *the great Pickwick… corridor*: A reference to Chapter XLI of *The Pickwick Papers*, and the comings and goings in the narrow, low, long and dirty corridors of the Fleet, the debtors' prison.

p. 28, *Philip Sidney*: The famous Elizabethan author of the *Arcadia*, a romance "adorned with beautiful poems", as Lampedusa was to write in his lessons on English Literature.

p. 28, *the birthplace of the proud mother of the great Oliver*: Elizabeth Stewart, the mother of Oliver Cromwell, was born in The Old Hall manor house in Stuntney, near Ely.

p. 29, *pale and angry rose*: A quotation from Shakespeare's *Henry VI, Part I* (Act II, Sc. 4, l. 107).

p. 29, *basinella*: Cotton fabric used for drapery.

p. 30, *as the man from Stratford would say*: A quotation from Shakespeare's *Sonnets* (LXXIII, l. 4).

p. 31, *En tout bien, tout honneur*: "With all good intentions", without any sexual designs (French) – an idiomatic expression often used by Molière: *Don Juan* (Act II, Sc. 2), *That Scoundrel Scapin* (Act III, Sc. 1), *The Miser* (Act IV, Sc. 1).

p. 31, *Lucien de Calenouvelle*: A joking French translation of "Lucio (Piccolo) di Calanovella".

p. 31, *the evil done to King Duncan*: A reference to Shakespeare's *Macbeth*.

p. 31, *Galanti… certainly himself*: A reference to Umberto Galanti, manager of the Hotel Villa Igiea in the Twenties.

p. 31, *The Monster's address… Whitby or Winchester*: The note is added, at the top, above the hotel's heading, on the recto of the fifth sheet.

V

My dear Casimiro,

The Monster finds himself in York once again! Because King George has had the noble whim to go and reside in Edinburgh for ten days and hold his court there, that city and all those around it are swarming with the most elegant and obstructive crowds, and the poor Monster, after a stay of two days in that magnificent city, has had to strike camp and complete a tour by car through the lochs and mountains of Scotland. Then, after a train journey during which he shone as a gifted and expert manipulator of railway timetables, he came back to York, whose Gothic windows, whose renowned hams, whose cream and cheeses, seem to be particularly congenial to the delicate physical constitution of the undersigned Monster.

The Monster will not linger over descriptions of Edinburgh and the Scottish countryside: that would be boring, and he is keeping it for the long winter evenings when he has nothing better to do. He must say however that he was sceptical about the attractions of the Scottish Highlands and has had to change his mind, since that area, although not very high, possesses a character which distinguishes it clearly from all other landscapes: its colours especially – the bright red of the heather, the innumerable shades of brown in the rocks, the dull greens of the pine trees, all of it frequently reflected and confused in the icy transparency of the lochs – are truly wonderful; and one can see that nature has been kindly disposed here and has managed to imitate to perfection the canvases of the great English and Scottish landscape painters.

At the very moment the Monster was leaving Edinburgh, your letter and Lucio's and the envelope containing the photographs were delivered to him, having been sent on from London.* The envelope containing the photographs was torn, and there were only four photographs in it – I do hope none of them have been lost. Ninuzzo's mistake* has not done any harm: letters with excess to pay are the only ones which always arrive at their destination.* And it isn't even as if the fragile finances of the Monster were disturbed, since the excess was paid by the hotel in London, English hotels regarding it as their duty and a point of honour not to put trifles like that on the bill – they are part of the hotel's budget, which has shoulders broad enough to bear this burden and many others too.

For the time being the photographs are resting in the bottom of the Monster's suitcase in the excellent company of a guidebook to Scotland, a book by Chesterton, and some bars of a special Edinburgh chocolate of which the Monster has thought it indispensable and pleasurable to make ample provision. (By the way it must be said that in Edinburgh the confectioners are particularly notable, and there is a *Waverley Tart* – composed of a light *pâte brisée*, dry cream, almond paste, slices of candied apricot and raisins – worthy of the utmost esteem.)

When the Monster returns to London – that is in a week's time – he will hasten to show your photographs to Sir Frederick Kenyon,* who is not only a *trustee*, that is a fiduciary, of the Wallace and director of the department of French antiquities at the Kensington, but also a gentleman graced with education, exquisite manners and extremely well-cut clothes. The Monster will complete the whole investigation with his usual sagacity, prudence and diplomacy. And that will be all the more pleasurable for him since this year he has not been to the Wallace, which is only a short distance away from his hotel (a short London distance: twenty minutes). The Monster would like to know if he may leave the photographs, should this be requested. He would like to have an immediate reply on that matter (Hôtel Great Central, Marylebone Road, London N.W.).

As for the *pupi*,* he will do what he can, in London. They are half life-size, without supports, and seem (to the layman) perfectly articulated, as some twenty of them were displayed and arranged in such a way that they looked as if they were playing a game of football, in all the awkward poses which that game involves. If you send the names of the firms, which you must know, it will be best.

I had forgotten to mention that in Lincoln, on the outside of the cathedral, the Monster has had the good fortune to come across a sculpture representing Mah-Jong – a thoughtful, pensive Mah-Jong and one apparently in love, whom the inhabitants of Lincoln, with keen perception, call "*Stinkie*", that is "foul-smelling".* It acts as an ornament for the Cathedral, and symbolizes I don't know what sinister demon or unnatural sin. The resemblance was so strong that the Monster immediately smelt the odour of sewers and swamps, and was about to blame the innocent municipality of Lincoln when he became convinced it was a case of autosuggestion, and that his nose had wanted to take part too in what his eyes had recognized. The Monster has a postcard of it. It is strange that your letter, which reveals a strong preoccupation with Gothic windows, reached the Monster precisely here at York, in whose cathedral there are in fact some of the most ancient and famous windows in the world. And what counts for more, in this particular cathedral several ancient kings were crowned, and hence it is perhaps the ideal background for the clumsy adventures of your little king. Pictorially, your notion seems to me very pleasing, and a good way of mitigating the incongruity of the subject matter; but from a lowly realistic point of view it is impossible, because these ancient windows do, of course, let the light through, but they are *matt*, and since from the inside one cannot see the outside, I imagine it would be more difficult from the outside to see inside, given the feeble light in the church. Anyway, it is not important. I am sending you some postcards which may help you to adapt the composition to the surroundings. If I had known beforehand that you were still on the first story, I would have sent you, from Lincoln, where there is a vast collection, some photographs of original ornamental Gothic motifs which would have been useful to you for the frames.

The postcards I am sending are not very beautiful: and the one in colour does not manage at all to convey the enchantment of that window of the *Five Sisters*, which is the most beautiful in the cathedral. The best is the one which shows the cross-vaulting of the church with its magnificent cluster piers and its lofty arches.

Lucio writes me a letter full of bawdy allusions: I think he wants to be paid back in his own coin – and he will not have to wait long for this. Meanwhile I can tell you that yesterday evening I thought about him a lot while I was going through Glasgow and reading in the guidebook that in that great port there are 173,000 people belonging to the dockers' union, a branch of the workforce which, because of their essential sturdiness, has always been a favourite of the *Chevalier de Calenouvelle*.*

I hope to leave the day after tomorrow for Liverpool (there must be many dockers there too!), where I shall stay only one day, but where there is one of the finest galleries of ancient and modern art in the whole kingdom.

I shall then go to Chester, Birmingham, Stratford-upon-Avon, Oxford and finally London.

The Monster is grateful for your long and agreeable letter, especially when he considers how little time you wish to devote to correspondence (at least to that with the male half of humanity), hopes you'll get really fat and stops now with greetings,

The well-fed Monster.

The postcards will not go in the letter and they are being sent separately.*

NOTES

On paper headed "Royal Station Hotel, York". Four sheets, eight sides. The letter is not part of the Fondazione Biblioteca di via Senato's collection, but is to be found in the Archives of the Fondazione Famiglia Piccolo di Calanovella at Capo d'Orlando, and has been published previously in *Archivio Storico Famiglia Piccolo di Calanovella*, edited by Anna Maria Corradini (Palermo, 2002). The text, collated with a photostat, is reproduced here with the inclusion of passages which were omitted and the elimination of mistakes made in the previous transcription.

p. 36, *your letter and Lucio's... sent on from London*: In his letter Casimiro Piccolo asks Lampedusa to obtain a valuation of a Sèvres tea set, owned by the Piccolos, of which he sends him photographs. The request for this appraisal should be seen in the context of the family's financial crisis, caused by the "*père prodigue*" (see Letter XIII). The matter of the Sèvres tea set will be the subject of other letters from Giuseppe (VII, VIII and IX). Together with the letter from Casimiro, there is also one from Lucio which – as can be inferred from what Lampedusa writes further on – contains what are presumably the usual insinuations on the sexual proclivities of various people in their coterie.

p. 36, *Ninuzzo's mistake*: Ninuzzo was probably one of the Piccolos' servants.

p. 36, *the only ones which always arrive at their destination*: A remark which is in a way prophetic: in 1954 Lucio Piccolo sent Eugenio Montale his first publication, *9 liriche*, and Montale was to say later that he had been impelled to read Piccolo's poems by the fact that he had paid excess amounting to 180 lire, since the postage of thirty-five lire was insufficient.

p. 37, *Sir Frederick Kenyon*: Frederick George Kenyon was an antiquary and papyrologist, and the director of the Wallace Collection.

p. 37, *pupi*: Puppets (Sicilian).

p. 37, *Mah-Jong... foul-smelling*: See note to p. 15.

p. 39, *Chevalier de Calenouvelle*: Lucio Piccolo (see second note to p. 31).

p. 39, *The postcards... are being sent separately*: The note is written slantwise on the verso of the fourth sheet.

VI

The Monster has written.

Making an enjoyable but by no means slight effort, limiting at times his liberty of action, always with the sacrifice of his means, the Monster has continued to write. He has poured out the treasures of his wisdom, of his culture, he has made all the facets of his polyhedric personality sparkle out. And that while he explores unknown and obscure lands among many vicissitudes, among the hundreds of snares set for the traveller by an unreliable climate, porters, railway workers and hoteliers.

The Monster has written.

And you, you swine, even among all the comforts of an epicurean existence, you who enjoy the strongest sunshine in Europe – one having no other occupation but to try to learn the Italian language, of which he is ignorant,* and the other castrating Wilde's stories and drawing chaste images from them to present to youngsters at an age when they are accustomed to fulfil the most elaborate fancies of a poet famous for many of his verses* – you, I say, have not been able for one moment to take your minds off your daily profanation of the arts to reply to the Monster, to the poor Monster who is far away, alone, wandering.

41

I repeat – swine.

The worn-out Monster has now found temporary respite in London, a place he has always considered calming
and restorative: he is happy to have completed his splendid
journey, in the course of which he has seen many beautiful
things and has greatly enriched his treasures of experience
and knowledge. He will show the photographs to the person
in charge,* but he will not send an account of the visit until
he has received your news.

And now the Monster is going to bed; he has an enormous
bed in which, although he is young and passionate, he sleeps
alone.

The Offended Monster

NOTES

On paper headed "Hôtel Great Central, London, N.W. 1". Two
sheets, three sides. In a space in the heading, between the name
of the hotel and the name of the city, Lampedusa has added the
address: "Marylebone Road".

p. 41, *one having no other occupation… ignorant*: Lucio Piccolo.
p. 41, *the other… verses*: Casimiro Piccolo.
p. 42, *show the photographs to the person in charge*: See first
note to p. 36.

VII

The Monster begins another monumental letter.

Yesterday evening the Monster received a letter from you, rich in Attic salt* and precious information, which arrived at just the right moment, because it provides some clarity regarding the photographs of the crockery. The Monster possesses five photographs, namely: 1) the trademark 2) the tray 3) one cup 4) one saucer 5) the coffee pot. He thought that this was the entire service, but he has learnt that there are also a milk jug and a sugar bowl (and, apparently, a second cup). And so this morning, Saturday, the Porcelain Monster put on his most elegant clothes, took the photographs (which he had previously taken care to enclose in a new and decent envelope), and *lento pede** he headed for the Wallace Collection, in the bright morning sunlight. He went through part of Marylebone, turned right into Baker Street, which he followed for almost the whole length, paused for a long time in Portman Square in obedience to the paternal orders of the *policeman* and also to the more imperious ones of his instinct for self-preservation, then he turned into a nondescript little street which led him into Manchester Square; there he went round the side of the central garden, thick with lime trees, and

43

eventually found himself in front of the building housing the museum. He climbed the five steps up to it, deposited his hat and stick in the foyer, and asked a well-fed attendant if Sir Frederick Kenyon* was in his office. Thus he was informed that that learned man is at present occupied in a journey through Poland, but that in the office there was another gentleman (with an incomprehensible name) who was filling in for him. The Imperturbable Monster extracted a visiting card from his pocketbook and asked the sleuth to convey it to the temporary master of the establishment. So it was that in a few moments he found himself in the presence of the most adorable of all old English gentlemen, with an antique-brick complexion and thick grey eyebrows above two childlike eyes, and adorned with long, flowing snow-white whiskers – all wonderfully groomed and redolent of Pears soap. He was elegantly dressed in a very heavy grey material with multicoloured pinstripes, generously cut, and on his shining black-leather shoes the white spats were gleaming in immaculate splendour. A red-and-yellow rose *panachée** enlivened his buttonhole, while his tie repeated, in more sober shades, the colour scheme of his clothing. He was standing upright, this Charon of the French eighteenth century, behind a large and unattractive but valuable boulle writing desk, and his head was softly haloed by an Aubusson tapestry; the silken curtains gently filtered the rather greenish light of the nearby trees; in the distance roared the incessant frenzy of the London streets.

In no way intimidated by such a noble vision, the Monster opened the conversation in clear Elizabethan English: "Sir," said he, "I would never have dared usurp the time, which is no doubt precious, of a *gentleman* I did not have the honour to be acquainted with, if my personal acquaintance with Sir

Frederick and the invitation he gave me to visit him here had not infused me with this, perhaps excessive, boldness."

The old gentleman smiled benignly: "Friends of Sir Frederick are also my friends; please tell me how I can be of service to you." And so speaking, with great courteousness, he extended to the Monster a box of cigarettes and invited him to be seated; and the tender bottom of the Monster bore down on the faded *Savonnerie* of an armchair of obvious authenticity. Having lit his cigarette, the Monster took out the photographs and displayed them, explaining how they depicted a Sèvres service belonging to one of his friends, which included, besides the pictured items, also a second cup, a milk jug and a sugar bowl, all of it in a marvellous and rare state of preservation, as indeed he could himself judge from the photographs; and he added that its owner would be pleased to know the real value of the service from a supreme authority like the management of the Wallace. The Monster, given the surroundings, judged it superfluous, ill-mannered indeed, to comment on or explain the trademark, comments and explanations which in any case the elegant gentleman himself immediately provided in his own identical terms. On seeing the photographs, the eyes of the noble old gentleman lit up with the ardour of a collector, and he examined them for a long time in a silence interrupted only by stifled moans of approval. Then he said that they were undoubtedly Sèvres and of the best period – and, as far as he could judge, in an exceptional state of preservation; he gave the familiar explanation of the trademark and, seized with sudden enthusiasm, he got up and with the photographs in his hand he invited the Monster to follow him. Through many corridors and up some stairs they got to a room, closed to the public, where they keep some pieces of the collection which are cleaned and reserved for detailed study by specialists. Here the Monster was shown a coffee service with an identical number of pieces, with an identical trademark, differing only in the themes depicted on them; and the old gentleman said that this was one of the best pieces in the collection, a present from Marshal Richelieu to one of his innumerable mistresses, and the Museum possessed a complete *pedigree*, that is the extremely detailed letter in which the Marshal ordered the service from the manufacturers, the letter with which the Marshal accompanied the gift, and finally the settled bill – things which apparently, both for the notoriety of the people involved and for the existence of the documents, greatly increase the value of the items. Then the old gentleman asked if (as it were) my service possessed anything similar – to which the Monster replied that he had heard that documents did exist, but that he was not in a position to say anything definite about them, and he asked him if he could say anything about the value of the service itself. In reply he said that simply on the basis of a photograph it was rather difficult, because from photographic reproductions he could only judge by the period and the excellent state of preservation, while the monetary value depends too on various other factors – colour, relief and provenance – of which he could not judge. And he led me into another room where he had a showcase opened and, in front of the astonished visitors, showed me two large twin Sèvres vases and invited me to take them in my hands and feel them. The terrified Monster (thinking of Fulco's mishap)* did that, and the wise Mentor pointed out to me how the network of gold and the figures were more perceptible under the thumb on one vase than on the other (a very slight difference apparently, because to the Monster they seemed equally smooth) – and he explained how, although they belonged to the same series and make, and were probably made the same day, if they had to be sold separately, one would fetch twice the price of the other. Then, with regard to the colour, he showed me various examples, in some of which the intensity of the colour added to their value while in others it diminished it. He embarked on subtle disquisitions which, while they convinced the Monster of his great competence, made him also realize what a complicated branch of knowledge Sèvrology is, and made him plumb the depths of the stupidity of Masnata,* who wants to deal with the great London antiquaries.

However, the Monster led the old gentleman back onto the right and interesting track of the price, and forced him to say that, even supposing (*by way of hypothesis*) that the photographs represented the most deficient product of Sèvres in the stated year, *the value of the service* (2 cups with saucers, tray, coffee jug, milk jug and sugar-bowl) *could not in any event be less* (if the authenticity was established) *than 600 pounds sterling* (55,000 lire at today's rate of exchange); that if all the necessary specifications of relief, colour, finish of the figures and documents were available, the value could increase to such an extent as to reach comfortably and even surpass four times that amount, that is *220,000 lire*. This was, he warned, a completely friendly and personal estimate, since a serious estimate could not be made on the basis of photographs. And this, he added, was the presumed *real* value, that is that which the item was worth in itself or in an auction for collectors, since any object *offered* or sold to dealers diminished in price; and it was the value *at the moment*, because in this kind of

47

thing prices fluctuate greatly according to how many are on the market. He added that the Wallace, possessing an almost complete collection of Sèvres, had not been buying any more for a long time; they were in fact not buying anything, except some paintings. The Monster then asked him if it would be worthwhile going to Christie's (the great auction house) to get another estimate: he said that was pointless; that no dealer would give firm estimates on the basis of photographs; he gave me to understand that the best expert was himself and that all that I could hope for was this estimate, a friendly one and in no way binding, and coming from someone who was disinterested; and he warned me to be careful, and if I went to antiquaries for estimates, this is what would happen: first of all, they did not give an opinion on the basis of photographs, but even if they did give an opinion, if I said that I did *not* wish to sell, they would give an exaggeratedly high estimate and then send the bill for the estimate, to be paid for as a percentage of the estimated value, a large bill and annoying to have to pay because it was superfluous and based on a fictitious valuation; if they gathered that one wished to sell, they would pitch their prices very low. He concluded: the value, as far as can be judged from photographs, was within the limits indicated; the estimate was quite personal and should in no circumstances constitute a precedent or a point of reference because, strictly speaking, a public gallery cannot give estimates of precious objects; it can serve only to let your friend know the *limits* of the value of his object and not to let himself be deceived; because if he does not wish to sell, that is enough; if he does wish to sell, he should package the items carefully and show them to experts who are, after all, numerous in Italy and as good as any others;

for example, he said, at the Poldi Pezzoli in Milan and the Floridiana in Naples;* not counting the supreme authority of the management of the present manufacturers of Sèvres – and that was only keeping within the range of public collections. His advice was always to avoid professional antiquaries, who either lower the estimate or raise (for their own reasons) exaggerated hopes. After which, this amiable and very cautious wise old man lit a cigarette, in defiance of museum regulations the whole world over, and took me to see other very fine objects, and delivered other learned discourses without any relevance to your service.

And so the Monster has done his duty. He has the photographs at your disposal: if you wish, he will carry out more researches, and he hopes he has been clear and eloquent in his account.

*　*　*

The Monster would now like to resume and conclude his account of the last phase of his journey. He must first, however, get two personal matters out of the way.

The first and more serious one concerns Lucio Gramma- tico (the worthy masculine form of Emma Grammatica).* The Monster has been the object of a relentless campaign of denigration by him; he regrets this and laments it. Not that he is afraid: since he is faced with low and sinister calumnies, he raises (he is entitled to say this) the monument of his own unblemished life utterly dedicated to a passionate search for truth. He does however regret that his efforts directed towards the moral redemption of one of the greatest sinners of all time are not appreciated; as is testified by a pamphlet which the said Monster has discovered in a knick-knack seller here, printed in 1601 with the title:

"Lives and deeds of notorious pederasts
being a most faithful account of the base lusts
of sundrie gentlemen of name;
and containing a most accurate tale of the foul loves
of Faulkes, duke of Vegetables, and Lucius of Newport
His acknowledged master-mistress."

Printed, by permission, in the Citie of London,
By Ronald Jehan, Lincoln's Inns.
MDCI*

And when the Monster does everything possible to make sure that the scandal – which has been going on for centuries and which even Saint-Simon* has discussed in immortal pages – should cease once and for all, he is attacked with reproofs, insults and threats.

From now on he will keep silent and let everyone stew in his own juice.

The second personal matter: the stained-glass windows. Faced with the miraculous explanation, the Monster rests his case. He cannot refrain from observing, however, that by the same reasoning it will possible one day to write a poem in which Mah-Jong's breath will be compared to the scent of Persian roses, and the fragrance of his armpits to myrrh, and the sweat of his feet will be transformed into intoxicating sandalwood ointment.* Miracles can do anything, even this – although after that one of arresting the course of the sun this would certainly be the most notable of all. He could make other observations, but he does not wish to give himself a reputation (or increase his reputation) as a pedant; and so he abstains, confident moreover that the watercolour must be very graceful and accurate.

* * *

And so after Liverpool the Monster went to Chester, where he spent a truly enjoyable day going through that city, which is so ancient and graceful and so well situated that it is a real jewel, one which no visitor to England should omit from his itinerary.

Afterwards, Stratford-upon-Avon. What struck him most there was the remarkable and truly divine gentleness of the countryside, a worthy source of such noble lyrics;* he has, in the moonlight, gone through the woods along the swollen and yet peaceful river, and he expected every moment to see lovable imps burst out, merry sprites like Puck, or adorable huntresses like the immortal Rosalind.* Nothing of this sort was seen – but silvery reflections on the waters, the rustling of squirrels among the leaves, the distant bleating of sheep: the immortal Shakespearean pastoral was born here, clearly. And far out of town, in a hidden nook, he even saw two lovers accomplishing the ultimate rites of love – and he was not scandalized, considering how this would have had the benevolent approval of the great William, quick to pardon human weaknesses as are all truly lofty and serene spirits. The little town is beautiful too, with many Elizabethan houses, including that New Place where the poet closed his eyes on this world, whose appearance he had transformed. Much peace, much serenity, much light. How different all that is from that tragic Ravenna, where his only other kindred spirit came to rest!* The tomb is an ugly thing but moving; the church on the contrary is downright magnificent, Norman, standing proudly on the bank of the gentle river, and surrounded by the most agreeable graveyard, all in the shade of age-old trees and overgrown with crimson wild roses twisting round the final crosses.

The Monster stayed in the Shakespeare Hotel, exquisitely furnished in the Elizabethan style – truly marvellous surroundings – the rooms are not numbered, but are named after characters in the plays. The Monster was given the "Falstaff room", which delighted him because it was a very good omen and the proprietor clearly meant to flatter him.

Then Oxford. It is one of those rare cities, like the incomparable Vicenza, and Siena, in which *everything* is beautiful. And the Monster cannot describe the immense delight he felt in walking among the noble buildings of amber-coloured stone, discovering at every step doors, courtyards, gardens, spires and façades full of graceful strength and venerable learning.

And the Monster was not surprised that from such surroundings, from Oxford and from Cambridge, *gentlemen* come forth.

After two days in Oxford passed in the deepest ecstasy and (it must be said) luxuriously lodged and fed in the Randolph Hotel, the Monster at 7 in the evening happily plunged back into London, like a whale into the ocean. And at 8 he re-emerged from his hotel, tidied up, shining and ironed, in "tails" that were clean if not impeccable, and he went off to dinner at the Ritz, a luxury he allows himself every now and then because he loves rare dishes and the spectacle of bare feminine shoulders in the soft light.

Cinemas. During this year the Monster has discovered some new cinemas, and this time they are grand and luxurious ones. No exceptional films, but several light and very amusing little comedies. He recommends, if you get the chance, those films which feature the actor Monte Blue, a very charming comedy (in the style of the famous *Midnight Visitors*) called *You'd Never Believe It*, and especially one featuring that comic actor Douglas McLean (which we saw only once and which we liked) entitled *Hold that Lion* – I don't know how they would translate it, but if you see publicity for films featuring Douglas McLean which have to do with lions, then go there, for it's really entertaining.*

The Monster sends his thanks and regards to Gaffiers;* he has also written to him personally. However, his affection does not lead him to commit himself just to please him and give a justification for his nomination as correspondent in Palermo, a nomination which is a sign of great prodigality on the part of the management of the newspaper.

The Monster will see to the puppets: and to the addresses of antiquaries – the Monster would be grateful for news, the Monster is tired and sends his regards

The Monster with a monogram on his rear.

NOTES

Seven lined sheets, thirteen numbered sides. In the top right corner of the first-sheet recto, the address written in pen and ink: "Great Central Hôtel Marylebone Road. / London. N.W. 1".

p. 43, *Attic salt*: Delicate wit, peculiar to the ancient Athenians.

p. 43, *lento pede*: "Slowly" (Latin).

p. 44, *Sir Frederick Kenyon*: See first note to p. 37.

p. 44, *panachée*: "Variegated" (French).

p. 46, Fulco's mishap: Probably the breaking of a vase. The reference is to Fulco Santostefano, Duke of Verdura, cousin and childhood friend of the Piccolos and the Lampedusas, and a companion in their intellectual pursuits. He left Palermo shortly after the First World War, and lived in Paris and New York. He worked with Chanel, and later devoted himself to designing jewels and opened his own factory in the United

States. He wrote *The Happy Sunny Days*, memories of his golden childhood in the Villa Niscemi ai Colli.

p. 47, *Masnata*: See first note to p. 6.

p. 49, *Poldi Pezzoli in Milan and the Floridiana in Naples*: A reference to the Poldi Pezzoli Museum of Art and the Villa Floridiana, which house large collections of ceramics.

p. 49, *Emma Grammatica*: A reference to the actress Emma Gramatica. "Grammatico" also means "grammarian", "scholar" or "pedant" in Italian.

p. 50, *Lives... MDCI*: The entire title-page inscription is in English. "Faulkes, duke of Vegetables" is Fulco Santostefano, Duke of Verdura ("Vegetables" in Italian). The insinuation of homosexuality is not without foundation. For Fulco Santostefano, see also first note to p. 46. "Lucius of Newport" is another burlesque translation Lucio di Calanovella's name. See also second note to p. 31.

p. 50, *Saint-Simon*: A reference to Louis de Rouvroy, duc de Saint-Simon, commonly known as Saint-Simon (1675–1775). In his *Memoirs* – which Lampedusa described as essential reading in his *History of French Literature* – Saint-Simon often lashed out at the depravity of French noblemen.

p. 50, *Mah-Jong's breath... sandalwood ointment*: See note to p. 15.

p. 51, *such noble lyrics*: Shakespeare's. He was born in Stratford-upon-Avon in 1564.

p. 51, *Puck... the immortal Rosalind*: Puck is a benevolent sprite from Shakespeare's *A Midsummer Night's Dream*. Rosalind (already mentioned in Letter I, p. 6) is a character from *As You Like It*.

p. 51, *Ravenna... came to rest*: Shakespeare's "only other kindred spirit" is Dante Alighieri, who died in Ravenna in 1321.

p. 53, *Monte Blue... entertaining*: Monte Blue (whose real name was Gerard Montgomery Bluefeather) was a famous American actor in the silent cinema, later taking on character roles. "*Midnight Visitors*" is *The Midnight Cabaret*, also known as *The Midnight Rounders* (1923), a comedy directed by and starring Larry Semon. *"You'd Never Believe It"* is *You Wouldn't Believe It*, a comedy directed by Erle C. Kenton (1920). Monte Blue is not in the cast. *Hold That Lion* was a 1926 comedy directed by William Beaudine, with Douglas McLean in the lead role.

p. 53, *Gaffiers*: A reference to the director of a Palermitan newspaper, either the *Giornale di Sicilia* or *L'Ora*. The nickname Gaffiers (from "gaffe") is an obvious allusion to his tactlessness.

VIII

The indefatigable Monster announces fresh developments in the matter of the tea service.

Yesterday morning (Sunday) the lazy Monster was still in his vast bed at 9, concentrating on the consumption of about a litre of milk, 6 rolls, 4 *toasts*, 4 slices of *cake* and some jars of jam, indispensable ballast for his daily sailing – when the telephone on top of his bedside table rang. And he was asked if he was the "Dewka di Palma", to which he assented, and at the other end it was said that it was the Wallace Collection on the line; they explained that Mr Albert Clay (the noble aged man of the previous day, evidently), before leaving the Museum yesterday, had arranged for me to be telephoned and to be told that they would like to have the photographs which I had shown him, *only those of the cups and saucers*, because he intended to take advantage of Sunday to compare them to certain books of his and show them to a friend. That if I would therefore put the photographs into an envelope, send them down to my porter, then a messenger would come from the Museum and take them and carry them to Mr Clay's place of residence.

When he had finished reading this message, they asked if and when the messenger could be sent. The Monster answered: "Immediately." He put *all* the photographs into an envelope, together with a note to remind them of the existence of the milk jug and sugar bowl, and sent them down to the *bureau*. And when, fully clothed and washed, he went downstairs, he learnt that they had already been taken. Then this morning a fresh telephone call: it was Mr Clay in person; the amiable man was profuse in his thanks and asked if the Monster could come to the Wallace between 11 and 12 to take back the photographs and speak with the same florid old man.

The Monster agreed. And at 11 $\frac{1}{4}$ he visited once more his wise Mentor, who was wrapped in reddish-purplish wool, with yellow shoes and a white rose. As always a real darling. He thanked me; he said that after a closer examination under a magnifying glass, and a comparison with other photographs and discussions with his friend, he was more and more convinced of the value of the pieces and especially of their quite exceptional state of preservation; and so he could *confidently* tell me that without doubt the minimum price that he had given yesterday was too low. He lamented the absence of photographs of the other two pieces, and seemed to be particularly anxious to know if the milk jug had feet or not – on which I could give him no information. It seems as if feet would be desirable. He appears to have had a discussion with his friend about the tray, which the friend thought was too small to hold the service and was also decorated in a different style, and therefore an odd item. Whereas the excellent old gentleman with sundry examples and subtle arguments convinced him after a long struggle (the memory of which still excited him) that everything was all right and that the smallness of the *plateau* (which is indeed obvious) was to be attributed to the different distances from which the photographs of the tray and the saucers were taken.

He concluded by giving some photographic advice *for the use of your friend*, saying that what gave him a right to do so was a long career spent in photographing objects in museums.

He said that the present photographs were all right and could remain as photographs of the details. That it would be desirable, however, to possess a series taken from exactly the same distance, by which the proportion the items bore to each other might be judged, even if this was to the detriment of the details. He also advised taking a photograph of the whole service, arranged on the *plateau*, with one of the cups in profile, in such a way that the shape and handles could be seen more clearly. And he added that it would be always useful to send, together with the photographs, the exact measurements of the single pieces and a concise history of the service. That was not for him, he said, who had by now formed an opinion, but in case one wished to show them to others.

After that he returned the photographs, and announced that on Thursday he was leaving for Scotland, and I went away.

But that is not all.

Yesterday evening the Monster dined with the Chief Officer Enrico Consolo, Director of the Commercial Bank, a Jew and a good man. He told him of his visit the day before to the Wallace and asked if he knew anyone who was an expert in porcelain.

The Consul said no. He was however a close friend of the celebrated Sir H. Witt,* celebrated as a famous advocate and as the owner of a valuable photographic collection of paintings, unparalleled in the world, of which even Venturi (senior)* has spoken to me this year, excited by its extraordinary interest (there are 200,000 items). This Sir H. Witt is a *trustee*, that is a fiduciary, of the National Gallery, and the Consul offered to give me a letter of introduction to him, because he in his turn knew all the collectors and antiquaries in London and would be able to set me on the right path.

This was written on notepaper from the *restaurant* itself, and it has today been left (with a visiting card and a request for an appointment) by the tireless Monster.

Now it is a matter of waiting on events.

Meanwhile the Monster will have to go away again shortly, and not to Paris but rather to North Wales, since he has received an invitation to spend 2 days at Palettopolis, that is at Powis Castle.* He is pleased at this, because now he will at long last see one of these famous castles. He will probably leave on 2nd August. With all these changes the Monster feels like a spinning top. Today the Monster has received a lot of correspondence sent on from York. In it was a postcard from O.S.* with a witty caricature and a curt line from Lucio.

With regard to the enchantment of Scotland, he would have many weighty things to say, but he hasn't even the time to catch a flea on his ample haunches.

He has also had a letter from the beloved Pupo,* which has produced those emotional effects which his (however plain) words never fail to have on the Monster's sensitive heart.

Erede is definitely engaged to be married. Walter is a ridiculous mad old fellow.*

The Monster will stop now, because he has to go and dress in elegant clothes to dine with a comely creature, who is as dear to him as ever (but always less than Pupo).

> The Monster, formed of delicate clay.*

NOTES

On paper headed "Hôtel Great Central, London, N.W. 1". Five numbered sheets, ten sides.

p. 59, *Sir H. Witt*: In the next letter he is given his correct name, Sir Robert Witt, solicitor and student of art.

p. 59, *Venturi (senior)*: Adolfo Venturi, father of Lionello, professor of art history at the University of Rome.

p. 60, *Powis Castle*: One of the most famous castles in Wales, with wonderful terraced gardens. The castle contains a collection of Indian objects gathered by Robert Clive, who had been governor of Madras (see also Letter IX).

p. 60, *O.S.*: Old Swine (see note to p. 15).

p. 60, *Pupo*: This reference has not been identified. He was (like Massimo Erede and Walter, mentioned immediately afterwards) one of a circle of Genoese friends. Pupo means "puppet" in Sicilian and can also be used as a term for a mischievous boy.

p. 60, *Erede... mad old fellow*: Massimo Erede, friend of Lampedusa, entertained him during his time in Genoa, and had probably been the connection between the writer and Genoa, the city where his first and only experience of publication began and ended (see Letter XVI, and the postcards and letters to Erede in the Appendix). He died young, missing in action during the Italians' retreat from Russia, and was the brother of the conductor Alberto Erede. The reference to Walter could not be identified.

p. 60, *formed of delicate clay*: The Sèvres service was from an early period, when porcelain was made from "delicate clay", and consequently more rare, because of the accidents to which this type of clay was subject during the firing. The effect of this delicate clay is softer, and it gives this period of Sèvres a characteristic background gentleness.

IX

The Monster, although he is rejected more and more, continues his labours in relation to the infamous service.

This morning he at last managed to see the elusive Sir Robert Witt.* He (always elegant, lean, clean-shaven) received him in his lawyer's office, on a busy and gloomy street in the City. He examined the photographs and found them very interesting, even though, he said, they were not his kind of thing. He offered to write me a letter of introduction to several experts, but when I said I had seen Mr Clay he added that I had already interviewed the highest possible authority, and that there was no need to see anyone else. He advised me frankly not to go to any antiquary because, he said, they always charge for estimates and, according to the price mentioned by Clay, an estimate would certainly cost no less than 30 pounds, that is about 3,000 lire. Then he gave me very sharp advice on auction sales and sales to collectors, which would be too lengthy to repeat here.

After which, this agreeable man (it is always a pleasure dealing with the English: they are courteous and prompt, and their apparent stupidity is merely an immense and uncontrollable shyness) went to the safe and took out of it a leather envelope from which he pulled a large line drawing in sanguine. This was quite simply an authentic Michelangelo, a sketch for Adam in the Sistine Chapel, bought recently for 600 pounds by the National Art Collection Fund, of which Sir Robert Witt is president (on the subject of paintings he is, it seems, a world authority). He himself told me that he takes advantage of his position as president to keep the paintings or drawings for a few days before sending them to the museum.

This National Art Collection Fund is a society of art lovers having at its disposal enormous funds, which it devotes every year to the acquisition in England and abroad of paintings and drawings that are then presented to the museums.

I have seen, too, the illustrated report of last year's acquisitions, full of beautiful things, among which are the most sumptuous embroidered vestments from the Middle Ages, found in a vestry in Yorkshire.

With that the Monster concludes his own task.

* * *

You will have received from me a postcard from Powis Castle. The beauty of that castle cannot be imagined or captured in a photograph, and the park still less. The Monster, despite his scornful nature, was overwhelmed. The large halls with old wood panelling and their ceilings of moulded sixteenth-century *plâtre*; the secret stairways and the trapdoors; the series of terraces going down onto the lawns and up towards the coppices; the 300 does and stags in the boundless park; the Monster's bedroom with a canopied bed and marvellous furniture; the thousand relics of the past which make one so aware of the antiquity of the family; the absence of ghosts and the excellence of the cuisine – these are all subjects with which the Monster intends to occupy his winter evenings.

Nor can he now describe the Reynoldses, the Gains-
boroughs, the Rubenses and the van der Weydens which
shine there, not to mention the other family portraits –
lesser but always well done (and what frames!) – or the
Limoges enamels, or the very valuable Indian jewellery (a
complete service for the consumption of *betel* in gold and
diamonds, a jade and emerald flask, etc.) which were Lord
Clive's booty* when he conquered India for the English. All
this in the middle of limitless grounds (Lord Powis is the
biggest landowner in England), full of game (500 pheasants
in one day) and with three other fully fitted castles.

* * *

We are pale shadows of the true lords. We are poor and we
shall die poor.*

* * *

Paletto* is always dignified and most amusing: she has
shown herself to be in possession of extraordinary historical
learning, even of Italian events, and can talk about the Di
Benedetto brothers* of Palermo much better than me, who
hardly know that they exist.

Lord Powis* (who is a druid (!) – I shall explain some
other time) has thawed and, as happens with the English in
similar circumstances, he has shown himself to be cultured,
amusing and interesting: he has gone round the world in
a sailing ship, was 3 years in India as Governor of Bengal,
has hunted tigers, lions, polar bears and kangaroos, has a
passion for agriculture and in his lifetime has had more than
half a million trees planted on his land (as one can see!).

His son, Lord Clive,* is cheerful and (usually) not at all stupid after the first hour of conversation. He is coming to Palermo in the winter and has already been invited to play *poker*, which he adores. He ought to marry one of those girls of ours who are starving to death – but he does not wish to.

* * *

The Monster is leaving here on 11th or 12th; soon he will be in Italy.

And he would like some news. He now owns an English identity card too (you have to have one when you stay for more than two months). It is warm now even here.

The wise Monster.

NOTES

On paper headed "Hôtel Great Central, London, N.W. I". Five sheets (numbered 2 to 4), ten sides.

p. 65, *Sir Robert Witt*: See first note to p. 59.

p. 65, *Lord Clive's booty*: See first note to p. 60.

p. 65, *We are poor and we shall die poor*: See first note to p. 25.

p. 65, *Paletto*: Lady Powis (Violet Ida Evelyn Lane-Fox, Baroness Darcy de Knayth).

p. 65, *the Di Benedetto brothers*: The three Di Benedetto brothers – Raffaele, Giulio and Salvatore – took part in the expedition of the Thousand. Raffaele was Garibaldi's aide-de-camp and is buried in the church of San Domenico, the so-called "pantheon" of Palermo.

p. 65, *Lord Powis*: George Charles Herbert, 4th Earl of Powis.

p. 66, *Lord Clive*: Mervyn Horatio Herbert, Viscount Clive.

X

The Monster, with a benevolence that verges on the ridiculous, continues to write.

This chapter *is dedicated* to Lucio the theologian.

A few days ago he read in the newspapers that the coming Sunday (now last Sunday) would be the first time in Anglican churches that the new prayer book would be used, the fruit of a recent revision with Catholic tendencies recently adopted after very lively and interesting discussions which the Monster followed with great attention, and of which the echo may perhaps have reached as far as the provincial shores on which you sit (and sweat). And so the Monster, moved by that noble intellectual curiosity which makes him akin to Goethe and Cestertonio,* went last Sunday to St Margaret's Church at the time of the service in order to be present at such an event, a more important one than might at first appear.

The heretical service proceeded peacefully and with great reverence up to a certain point, but when the celebrant read a few words concerned with a new interpretation of the Eucharist, a murmur ran through the crowd. And about twenty people got up and assembled in one of the aisles, muttering; after which one of them left the group, advanced towards the clergyman, put his hand up like a schoolboy and asked to be allowed to speak. He declared that his conscience would not allow him to be present at a service which contained, according to him, interpretations contrary to the Scriptures, and that therefore he must, with his companions, withdraw.

The unfortunate clergyman, mortified by this undignified scene, offered to explain afterwards how the new service adhered to the sacred texts; the protester bowed and, followed by his group of followers, left the church.

Shortly afterwards the Monster – this descendant of austere saints and learned prelates – left too, affirming the supreme dignity of the Roman Church and whispering those definitive words of the immortal *abbé*: "*Les loups se dévorent entre eux tandis que les agneaux paissent en paix.*"*

This chapter is for Casimiro, the "paynter".

The Monster has been to the Tate Gallery to visit the new wing, recently built to house modern painters from abroad. There is an abundance of Manets, Monets, Degases, Renoirs, Gauguins, Pissarros, Van Goghs and Mancinis. There are plenty of ugly items – but the Monster must admit that Degas seems to him a great painter. And he cannot say why. But there is a whole room devoted to Sargent. The incompetent Monster cannot judge the technical skill of those portraits, all of which nevertheless seem to him remarkable, but if a painter's excellence consists in the depth of the scenes depicted, in an indiscreet understanding of the soul of the subject, and the projection of this soul onto canvas – then it must be said that Sargent was one of the greatest artists who have ever lived.

The nine portraits of the Wertheimer family, which seem to represent Sargent's masterwork,* are brought together in this room with the rest. The Monster sat down in front of them, and was as amused as if he had been in a theatre; because it really is like being at a play: these canvases are so profound, and the characters brought out so strongly; the metaphor of the "speaking likeness" is realized; and these portraits do not merely speak but they say what their subjects would never have dared to confess.

Daddy Wertheimer* (whoever he is) emerges in a *redingote* from a dark background, which must be the source of his fortune, with the merriest and most wicked piratical face that ever was; the bejewelled Mummy Wertheimer* is trying with her thin lips and black dress to play the grande dame, while stinking of the ghetto from a hundred miles.

With the daughters one can admire every variation of corrupt wealth: one, ugly and intellectual with her spectacles and white lead, could easily become a theosophist or an amateur anarchist; the other one is the good-humoured cow, perfumed and smutty, and unquestionably the lover of her *chauffeur*; and in the same painting can be seen also an odious brother, a sixteen-year-old youth, no doubt with clammy hands, and with an arrogant and doltish and sporty air about him;* I hate to say it, but with a striking resemblance to Raimondo Arenella.*

Then there is the elder brother* wrapped in an impeccable *redingote*; Sargent has here performed a miracle of intuition by not bringing out the character, since there is no character to bring out. The portrait seems unfinished, but it is not: the subject was unfinished, clearly the owner of racehorses and a great *lion* in his circle of Jewish millionaires. Then, to demonstrate the good faith of the painter and his lack of bias, the portrait of the third brother, on the other hand, shows the noble figure of a thoughtful and honest young man.* Other portraits show the young ladies in fancy dress, and innumerable children.*

I assure you that it is worth the effort to come to London just to see this.

The irony of it is that this series of portraits was donated to the gallery by Mr Wertheimer himself, blessedly unaware of the eternal shame he has laid himself open to – because on his portrait the word "thief" is to be read as if it were written in scarlet letters.

* * *

In a shop the Monster has seen some lovely gambling tokens in lightly engraved mother-of-pearl; they are moulded in a vaguely oriental style, in the shape of fishes, birds, shields and figs; the Monster also yearns to own them because he can imagine the varied and refined conversation which their shapes would provoke. But they cost a packet, very much more than the greatest fictitious value which they could have in gambling. And the O.S.* would pocket them.

* * *

The Monster, now that he is not occupied with worldly matters, is frequenting a series of luxurious cinemas; and since at every performance he has seen two *films*, he believes he has seen beforehand the entire 1929 film programme for Palermo. Nothing extraordinary, to tell the truth, but an effort towards a greater psychological interest, and in two or three *films* he found himself interested in the drama as a clash of characters. All of them new actors, and very skilled; more intimate themes, less spectacular and also less puritanical (finally some married ladies are seen with lovers); lots of unknown beauties among whom he recommends Josephine Dunn.* The *films* were accompanied by ingenious instruments that imitate noises, especially effective for stormy seas and rain; there are shootings but, wisely, they are muffled and not realistic like those frightful ones in *The Big Parade*;* the variety turns are always elaborate, with original stage-light effects, completely unknown among us. In contrast to Italy, the cheapest seats are, logically, the highest.

Here the Monster concludes his *London Gazette*.

He, who has now crossed Europe from south to north, from Palermo to Edinburgh, is getting ready to cross from west to east, from London to Bolzano. He will stay a very short time in France. He is leaving perhaps the day after tomorrow.

* * *

You really are swine not to write to me; it is however useless to do it now: in a few days you can write to Hôtel Caldaro – Passo della Mendola – (Alto Adige) –

The super-fed Monster.

71

NOTES

On paper headed "Hôtel Great Central, London, N.W. 1". On numbered sheets, twelve sides.

p. 67, *Cestertonio*: A humorous Italianization of G.K. Chesterton's surname.

p. 68, *Shortly afterwards... paissent en paix*: Some of Giuseppe Tomasi di Lampedusa's ancestors were indeed "austere saints and learned prelates". One of them, Cardinal Giuseppe Tomasi (1649–1713) was beatified in 1803 and made a saint in 1986. The French quotation, slightly adapted by Lampedusa, is from Anatole France's *The Queen Pédauque*: "'Amen,' *dit mon père. 'Les agneaux paissent en paix, tandis que les loups se dévorent entre eux.'*" ("'Amen,' said my father. 'The lambs graze peacefully while the wolves devour each other.'"). The sentence is addressed by Léonard Ménétrier, father of Jacques, the narrator and protagonist, to the "immortal" Abbé Jérôme Coignard. Abbé Coignard, a character much loved by Casimiro Piccolo and Lampedusa, appears also in another work by Anatole France, *The Opinions of Jérôme Coignard*.

p. 69, *seem to represent Sargent's masterwork*: In 1898, John Singer Sargent, the most acclaimed and sought-after portrait painter of the late Victorian period, was commissioned by Asher Wertheimer, a rich London art dealer, to paint portraits of himself and his wife on the occasion of their silver wedding. Wertheimer's portrait came to the Tate Gallery in 1922, as a legacy from Asher himself, together with eight other family portraits; his wife's portrait, on the other hand, is today in the New Orleans Museum of Art.

p. 69, *Daddy Wertheimer*: Asher Wertheimer.

p. 69, *Mummy Wertheimer*: Natasha Wertheimer, Asher's wife.

p. 69, *With the daughters... about him*: Lampedusa is describing the portraits of Hylda, Almina and Conway Wertheimer respectively.

p. 69, *Raimondo Arenella*: See second note to p. 6.

p. 69, *elder brother*: Edward Wertheimer.

p. 70, *honest young man*: Alfred Wertheimer.

p. 70, *Other portraits… innumerable kids*: Ena and Betty, Hylda, Essie, Ruby and Ferdinand, Almina in oriental costume, all children of Asher and Natasha Wertheimer.

p. 70, *O.S.*: See note to p. 15.

p. 71, *Josephine Dunn*: American actress. Born in 1906, she had already appeared in nine films, three in 1926 and six in 1927.

p. 71, *The Big Parade*: A 1925 film by King Vidor. One of the first films set during the First World War, it marked a decisive turning point towards realism and topicality in cinema.

XI

As promised, the Monster yesterday evening made a tour
of inspection in Rue du Colisée. This is a small street which
runs off the Avenue des Champs-Élysées immediately
after the Rond-Point, on the right going towards the Arch.
One of the buildings on the corner of this by now famous
thoroughfare is being demolished for reconstruction, which
for the moment spoils the effect of elegance which that
road, a true pearl oyster, ought to have. The other corner is
occupied by a graceful-looking building entirely taken over
by *Renée-robes-fourrures-manteaux* and is hence a hive of
little dressmakers, to whose charms, we hope, their shapely
neighbour will not remain insensible. As if that were not
enough for him, there is beneath a luxurious shop which
under the unexpected name of Byron deals in men's shirts,
socks, pyjamas and braces, and which must therefore be
provided with male staff and clientele. Just inside the street,
on the right, abutting on the demolition but, certainly by
the intervention of Apollo, not itself demolished, arises
the Hôtel du Colisée, of slight or rather paltry dimensions,
and of a great age, but endowed with an entrance which is
indescribably elegant and mysterious. Facing it is a small
avant-garde theatre, *le Studio des Champs-Élysées*, with a

75

cubist façade, closed at present. Farther along, the street plunges into limp mediocrity with a confectioner's, a baker's and other low establishments. Only some small *restaurants*, second-class but with their names revealing artistic aspirations, continue the tradition of elegant bohemianism with which the street begins.

* * *

The Monster is leaving again shortly for Dijon, a city which is dear at the same time to his artistic soul, his historiographical intellect and his stomach as a *gourmet*.

And on the 18th I will be in Bolzano.

At the Hôtel Caldaro – Passo della Mendola, he hopes to find some good news from you, and he wishes you to know that your epistolary conduct has been below any kind of reproach –

The Monster of the Elysian Fields

NOTES
On paper headed "Hotel Terminus Nord" of Paris. Two numbered sheets, four sides.

XII

The Alpine Monster greets you.

He has written a number of letters which, collected and printed, would make a substantial 8vo volume.

In these he has been witty, descriptive, profound and wise; and in them has shone every facet of an intelligence which has no equal in Europe nowadays.

All that without managing to squeeze from your dried-up pens even the tiniest drop of ink.

I see clearly – ah yes! – I see clearly that, as love breathed into Dante, so self-interest alone inspires you; and that, in order that I might see a few lines from you, I must wait until Casimiro has a yearning for some cigar-lighters, bacon-cutters and patented lemon-squeezers; that he uses the Monster as a means of squandering his ill-gotten savings. And yet it is precisely now that the Monster, among so many trees and rocks, and deprived of the vital food which London his nurse poured out for him, needs some distraction.

He encloses a list of London antiquaries, meticulously compiled, to be delivered to Masnata,* whose new address he does not know.

The Monster is about to change his abode, and if you ever, repenting of your sins, wish to write to him, you can do it to "Hôtel Post-Bemelmans".

(Bolzano) Collalbo sul Renon.

Best wishes,

The Monster smelling of resin

NOTES

One sheet folded in two, to make four sides. On the top of the first page the address: "Hôtel Caldaro / Passo della / Mendola". Slantwise, on the top left, the date.

p. 77, *Masnata*: See first note to p. 6.

XIII

[Collalbo,] 3rd September [1927]

The Monster is by nature compassionate and endowed with a tender heart – a weakness of which the wicked very often take advantage to inflict torment and suffering upon him; besides which, the scenes of nature all around are limpid and serene, as revealed in the gentle verdure of the woods and in the perennial striving of the treetops towards the peaceful sky, and the hotel's cuisine is delightful and would predispose anyone to mildness.

The Monster therefore pardons and absolves, but this is a long way from humiliating himself and imploring pardon, and he has decided not to do so.

He had, to tell the truth, anticipated the reason for such an obdurate silence, and this it was which kept the expression of his anger within bounds. But he really does deplore the embarrassing situation in which you are placed, and he hopes that a well-addressed burst of energy will serve to break this vicious and disastrous circle. *Le père prodigue* has emerged from Dumas's play and proceeds along the flowery ways of the Riviera of Genoa with the clear-cut features and structural finish which are more commonly the qualities of an artistic creation than of real life.*

And the unexpected apparition of the sacred shade of Pius X into all this business adds a note of subtle humour such as only a Dickens or a Cestertonio* could have thought up.

But, joking apart, that is all very sad, and I hope you'll be able to find a definitive way out.

The news Lucio has given me* has terrified me, without however arousing my indignation or surprising me. And I must say that, despite your repeated assurances, I have not yet managed to convince myself of its authenticity, and I hope that these are some of your elaborate deceptions which, with the agreement of Masnata himself,* you would like the ingenuous and trustful Monster to fall for.

But I propose to write on this matter at greater length to Lucio, and perhaps even today.

* * *

We are doing very well here, where we arrived only yesterday. The hotel is as charming as ever, furnished to excellent effect in a very modern way with sitting rooms in the Munich Secessionist style and beautiful gardens with sloping terraces. The cuisine, as I have mentioned, is exquisite and the clientele elegant. The climate is temperate, just as far from the tremendous heat of the plains as from the early snows of Mendola.

I am waiting for the promised letter, on which I am relying, and Mother and I send you affectionate greetings

The sylvan Monster

NOTES

One sheet folded to make four sides. On the top of the first page the address: "Hôtel Post-Bemelmans. / (Bolzano) / Collalbo".

p. 79, *Le père prodigue… real life*: *Le Père prodigue* (*The Prodigal Father*) is a comedy by Alexandre Dumas (*fils*). The father of the Piccolo brothers, Baron Giuseppe, had abandoned the family some time ago and was living in Sanremo with a ballerina, by whom he had children. Giuseppe Piccolo died in November 1928, but the resulting financial problems were starting to be worrying. After the death of her husband, Baroness Teresa sold the villa in Palermo (it stood at the corner of Via Libertà and Piazza Francesco Crispi), and on the site a residential block was built, which is still in existence. But the transaction did not resolve the situation and, in 1933, the Piccolos left Palermo and went to their country villa Vina at Capo d'Orlando. Lampedusa, with a note of admiration for Aunt Teresa, remembered that before shutting herself away in the country, Baroness Piccolo had said: "We have lost everything, but we will get everything back." In the early Fifties Teresa's stubbornness and willpower had achieved the result she had foreseen, and in his aunt's words, as Giuseppe remembered them, resounded the melancholy of Giuseppe himself, since he had gone in the opposite direction and, at the beginning of the Fifties, he could definitely say that he had lost everything.

p. 80, *Cestertonio*: See first note to p. 67.

p. 80, *The news Lucio has given me*: See the following letter.

p. 80, *Masnata himself*: See first note to p. 6.

XIV

Dear Lucio,

Your pen, so accustomed to sketching azure seraphim among woods of golden trees, has suddenly adopted the very harsh style in which those chapters in Genesis on the last days of Sodom were composed.

I am glad, among so much turpitude, that you realize the far-sightedness of the Monster, scrutinizer of souls and disciple of the infallible Revel.* But the Monster himself is now aware of living on the shores of a densely populated Dead Sea: the Monster and Pupo,* you and Fulco, Fulco and the whole world, Masnata's orgies, Filopene's minions and O.S.'s shepherd boys* make up a mob of satyrs and nymphs to put the metropolitan renown of Berlin or London to shame.

But I still do not want to believe in the accuracy of your information.

I was myself once in the notorious *garçonnière* on the Foro Umberto (ah! *foro!*),* but, apart from mounds of bureaucratic papers, I did not see anything there but a particularly ugly female typist and a chap making tortoiseshell frames, who seemed to me unlikely to arouse any lust. And I never would have believed that those bare

rooms, owned by Fofò* who is surely uncorrupted, could at
the nod of such a petty charmer as Masnata turn into the
grottoes of the Mincius or those drawing rooms of Mayfair
which saw the loves of Corydon and Dorian Gray.*

I guess you have not have handed him the list of London
antiquaries which I sent. And I beg you not to do that, lest
the police in any of their searches are given any reason to
believe I was passing on the addresses of over-jolly dens
under the guise of respectable antiquaries.

I am waiting for news of any developments in the affair,
and I can imagine, with horror, Mah-Jong's revolting joy* at
the announcement of the scandal.

Un libertinage si contraire à la volupté*...

I would not want, at the end of a letter full of such shame,
to talk about Rosalind* and her successive Anglo-Saxon
incarnations, but nothing forbids me to recommend to you,
just to raise your spirit to a higher level, *The Everlasting
Man* by Cestertonio,* in my opinion the noblest book of
Catholic apologetics since Manzoni, full of lofty poetry,
after reading which the redundant pages of Papini's *Christ**
look like the infantile blasphemy which they are –

The patristic Monster

NOTES

One sheet folded to make four sides. On the top of the first page
the address: "Hôtel Post-Bemelmans. / (Bolzano) / Collalbo".

p. 83, *the infallible Revel*: Bruno Revel, fellow prisoner with
   Lampedusa at Szombathely, son of a Waldensian priest and
   owner of a villa at Montepellice. He was Professor of French
   Literature at the University of Milan, and one of the people
   closest to Lampedusa in the Twenties.

p. 83, *Pupo*: See third note to p. 60.

p. 83, *Fulco... shepherd's boys*: For Fulco and Masnata, see note to p. 46 and first note to p. 6. Filopene (an expressive nickname, which can be rendered "Lover of the Penis") is Pietro Emanuele Sgadari di Lo Monaco (Bebbuzzo). See also note to p. 15. For O.S. see note to p. 15.

p. 83: *foro*: Foro Umberto I is one of Palermo's main thoroughfares. Lampedusa is here punning on the other meaning of *foro*, "hole".

p. 84, *Fofò*: This reference has not been identified.

p. 84, *the grottoes of the Mincius... Dorian Gray*: Literary examples of homosexual passion. "Mincius" and "Corydon" allude to the second of Virgil's *Eclogues* and the unhappy love of Corydon for Alexis, and also to André Gide's *Corydon*. The "drawing rooms of Mayfair" and "Dorian Gray" are references to Oscar Wilde's novel *The Picture of Dorian Gray*. Before "saw" Lampedusa had written, and immediately crossed out, "sheltered".

p. 84, *Mah-Jong's revolting joy*: For Mah-Jong, see note to p. 15.

p. 84, A quotation from Paul Valéry's *Au Sujet d'Adonis*: "*un libertinage si contraire à la volupté et si mortel à la poésie*" ("a libertinism so unpleasant and so deadly for poetry").

p. 84, Rosalind: See sixth note to p. 6.

p. 84, *The Everlasting Man by Cestertonio*: G.K. Chesterton's famous 1925 Christological essay. For "Cestertonio", see note to p. 67.

p. 84, *Papini's Christ*: A reference to *The Life of Christ* (1921) by Giovanni Papini, an essay influenced by its author's conversion.

XV

Lucio, crowned with laurel,
I was hoping to receive your news and with it fresh
particulars of the sodomite scandal, a marvellous subject
for discussion and meditation, I imagine, in that blazing tail
end of the Sicilian summer. But your epistolary flow is, I
see clearly, not merely intermittent but short-lived, and its
waters flow with the laboured sparingness of Valéry's lyrics.

That puts in a stronger and stronger light the magnificent
soul of Pupo* who, without occupation and sunk in
luxurious leisure in Genoa, engages me in a most active
correspondence, occasionally offering, with unheard-of
precision, details of his own and others' flirtations, in such
a way as to raise a blush on the most hardened chimpanzee,
not to mention the notoriously bashful Monster; at other
times compiling lengthy epistles, true *Moral Essays* in
which I continually grieve at not being able to discover the
humanist perfection of style of my famous cousin from
Recanati;* and in which with enviable lightness he passes
from the austere ethical speculations of Epictetus to the
facile cynicism and low worldly positivism of which the
impure source is Guido Veronese.*

87

* * *

The Monster is doing really well in this little town of abbeys, cloisters, powerful bishops and clear flowing waters and decorous hills. And he is reading and making shrewd annotations on the profound lyrics of the respectable Dean of St Paul's.*

I have learnt of the numerous tragic deaths which have gladdened the summer over there. O my cradle, O city of my childhood, why within the iron-coloured circle of your hills are you so filthy, sad and desperate? And why do you elect, as your perpetual inhabitants, Tragedy without a soul and Grief without any light?*

(This is a poetical periphrasis of the well-known saying: "A hell of a place".)

Hoping to hear news from you soon, respectful greetings from

The Rhaetian Monster.

NOTES

One sheet folded to make four sides. At the top of the first page the address: "Bressanone – Hôtel Excelsior –".

p. 87, *Pupo*: See the previous letter and third note to p. 60.

p. 87, *Moral Essays... famous cousin from Recanati*: A reference to Giacomo Leopardi and *Moral Essays*, a collection of philosophical dialogues. The Tomasi family and the Leopardi family have the same coat of arms and were reputed to be cousins.

p. 87, *Guido Veronese*: A reference to Guido da Verona, a popular Italian writer of the early twentieth century.

p. 88, *the respectable Dean of St Paul's*: John Donne.

p. 88, *O my cradle... without any light*: Many of the words used by Lampedusa in this paragraph are taken or adapted from Dante's *Inferno*.

XVI

[Bressanone,] 1st October 1927

The Monster (a simpleton of antediluvian grandeur) is being regaled with laurels of late.

He has received a letter from the notorious 3Ms telling him that Senator Corradini has written to 3Ms himself, congratulating him on the "marvellous" article (signed by the Monster) concerning Julius Caesar which appeared in *Le Opere e i Giorni* – and therefore the benign 3Ms is hastening to make the acquaintance of the Monster, the blissful mother of such a bonny baby.*

Then Raffaele Calzini sent the Monster, on charming notepaper headed *Corriere della Sera*, a letter of boundless courtesy and lavish (and deserved) praise. Glory begins to garland the head of the Monster, that divine youth.

All that has aroused in the innocent heads of my parents quite unfounded hopes and yearnings, and they already see me ensconced on page three of the *Corriere* as the fearful Minos of European letters, fattened on lavish offerings. The only practical result of this will be a journey by the Monster to Milan,* a month hence, without any particular aim but which may, with the admirable candour of the previous generation, be summed up in the phrase "infiltrate into the *Corriere*" – all of it of course ending up with several risottos and some pastries at Cova's.* A further result is the renewed energy with which the Monster is working on his heavy-going and pointless article on Cestertonio,* a task beyond his powers, but which he hopes to finish and send to the coveted 3Ms when he goes to Genoa in November, on a noble literary mission which, however, will also include other delightful and more desirable amusements.

In Genoa, meanwhile, there is some news: *Le Opere e i Giorni* is expanding at an amazing rate with injections of capital and subscriptions; Erede is engaged to a girl much less desirable and desired than that of his rival, Pupo.*

Pupo is out of work and has become rich, learned and decidedly cracked; his incomparable ex-fiancée writes to the Monster every now and then with her irresistible farrago of naivety and licentiousness. The busy 3Ms is slothfully fumbling about in his millions.

It is a short distance from him to Fulco,* and I shall travel it. I am glad that he has come to liven up the decline of that Palermitan summer of yours – still blazing and blighted by the sirocco, from what I am told – and that, in order to see once more the old places and no-longer-young friends, he has given up the radiance of *la plage du soleil et des pyjamas** (as, not without a touch of cheesiness, we read in the *réclames* for the Lido). Lucio, particularly, will rejoice in this, and I am convinced that it is only for the sake of politeness that he places him second in the list of his favourites, after a certain "lofty spirit" who is unknown to me.

As I fix my gaze on Lucio's style, which is as lucid as ebony, it seems to me that Masnata's judicial problems* are turning out for the best, although some episodes of a private and not entirely exemplary nature are emerging. The Monster had always put him first among candidates for the gallows; I would like to hope that, after such convincing proof of his powers, you will accord him an eminent position among psychologists, at least by the side of Casimiro who, because of his occupation as portrait painter, is endowed, as everyone knows, with an uncommonly penetrating mind.

The utter peacefulness of this delightful little town was broken some days ago by floods. A slow and gentle rain – which lasted, however, for 24 hours – swelled all the local torrents, which in their turn swelled the Isarco which, shaking off its peaceful sky-blue look of normal days, became sludgy and foamy, with huge, violent, sea-like waves bearing along innumerable tree trunks, household scraps and corpses, and striking the bridges and the banks like a mangonel, with a truly tremendous roaring and howling. It looked for a moment as though the city had run into serious danger, and the Monster were about to swim through the waters like Leviathan.

Fortunately the rain stopped, the fury of the elements died down, and now everything is back to normal – but not without leaving some twenty victims of a nearby railway accident, and serious destruction, with all the local bridges damaged and closed to traffic, the weaker ones having disappeared. The Monster, from the safe viewpoint of a hill 50 metres above the level of the river, observed the spectacle, thus adding new gems to the rich coffer of his experience.

The Monster thanks you for the interest shown by Casimiro in his appetite: it is excellent, and very well catered for by Signor Schachner, the egregious proprietor of the hotel, and not by the Alpine meadows, as has been tendentiously insinuated. Best wishes –

The famous Monster

NOTES

Two numbered sheets of lined paper, four sides. On top left corner of the first page, the address: "Bressanone – Hôtel Excelsior –"; and below, in brackets: "the Monster's address from now on is: Hôtel Stiegl – Bolzano".

p. 89, *He has received a letter... bonny baby*: "3Ms" is a reference to Mario Maria Martini, director of the magazine *Le Opere e i Giorni*. Enrico Corradini was a journalist, the founder and director of the magazine *Il Marzocco*, a senator and a member of the Fascist Grand Council. Lampedusa's article was a review of *Caesar: Geschichte seines Ruhms* (1924) by Friedrich Gundolf.

p. 89, *Raffaele Calzini... to Milan*: Raffaele Calzini was a writer and journalist. Calzini's letter, dated 24th July 1927, was preserved by Lampedusa, and it reads: "Dear Sir, It is only today that I have received your address and can do what I have had in mind for a long time and send you a word of thanks. A very fine article signed by you, which appeared in the magazine *Le Opere e i Giorni*, gave me the inspiration for a short story published some months ago in the *Corriere della Sera*. The story was entitled *The Emperor and the Scribe*, and the article was a review containing a perfect summary of a German book on the fame of Julius Caesar. Thank you for that, and please give my regards to beautiful Palermo if you are there and the Prince of Trabia if you chance to meet him. Faithfully, Raffaele Calzini". There is no mention of an invitation to Milan.

p. 90, *Cova's*: The confectioner's near the Teatro alla Scala, made famous by writers such as Hemingway and Soldati.

p. 90, *heavy-going and pointless article on Cestertonio*: The article on Chesterton never appeared in *Le Opere e i Giorni*.

p. 90, *Erede... Pupo*: For Erede and Pupo, see third note to p. 60.

p. 90, *Fulco*: See note to p. 46.

p. 90, *la plage du soleil et des pyjamas*: "The beach of sunshine and pyjamas" (French).

p. 90, *Masnata's judicial problems*: See Letter XIV and first note to p. 6.

XVII

"The Monster"
A company specializing in the supply and repair of testicles
— By appointment to the Bellini Club —

Florence, 16th November 1927 — Anno VI*

Dear Sir,

The usual ill-wishers have spread the rumour that our ancient and highly esteemed firm was out of stock of those articles which for many years it has had the honour of supplying to its valued and distinguished clientele. Such rumours are completely unfounded, and we reserve the right, if necessary, to take legal action against those who circulated them. Our *stock* of testicles, bollocks, cojones, nuts, balls and *mah-jongs** is always extensive, and we are able to satisfy promptly the needs of any client.

Having been apprised by you of your desire to be supplied by our firm, we have the honour to forward our list of the various models available in our warehouse, and a few testimonials out of the many thousands in our possession.

Consequent to the revaluation of the lira, the prices marked are subject to a discount of 20%. Cash on delivery of the goods. Postage and packing at the purchaser's expense.

In the anticipation of numbering you among our clients, we send you our kindest regards,

"The Monster"

"The Monster"
Company specializing in the supply and repair of testicles.
   By appointment to the Bellini Club.

Catalogue and list of prices
for 1927 (Anno VI)

Testicles of the *Excelsior* quality, guaranteed for ten years; stove-enamelled, bright red, of the greatest potency. As used by royalty.

L.12,000 the pair.

The *Excelsior* model is infallible even in the most refractory cases, and is particularly suitable for decadent poets and Pizzetti-like musicians.*

Testicles of the *Vertex* quality, guaranteed for ten years, with autogenous welding, neutral colour, medium strength.

L.10,000 the pair.

The Vertex model offers, at a lower price, all the advantages of the other more expensive devices. Its neutral colour will be appreciated particularly by gentlemen who are painters, since it gives them the opportunity to display, in decorating them, all the riches of their palettes.*

Testicles of the *Valencia* quality, guaranteed for five years, designed expressly for special tasks, with triple nickel-plating and replaceable parts.

L.5,000 the pair.

Our firm is so perfectly organized that we are able to offer these items at the lowest possible prices, such as to beat any competition. We have delivered large consignments to several entomological societies, by whom they are appreciated for their resistance to moths and for being acid-proof.* Keep them well away from incubators.

Testicles of *La Ménagère* quality – with a two-year warranty, burnished, with coil springs.

L.2,000 the pair.

We hope that our valued customers will find what they need among these various items. The packaging is attractive and very sturdy, and every piece is accompanied by detailed instructions on its application and use, with several illustrations.

"The Monster". Testicle suppliers.

A selection of our testimonials:

Palermo, 20th August 1927 (Anno VI)

Dear Sirs,

I wish to register my profound satisfaction with the *Vertex* appliances, which I have been using for two years without impediment. As a consequence of the fresh energy they have given me, in only six months I have managed to complete a watercolour with an area of 16 square centimetres representing "Eumolpus and Giton in bed",* a somewhat risqué subject which I have however been able to treat without any offence to modesty or decency, showing them as two bald old men with spectacles intent on reading the newspaper and clothed in steel shorts. The neutral colour of the testicles that have been wisely chosen by them has enabled me to decorate them in watercolours, in a combination of violets, opals and reds (Gothic stained glass) which I think has turned out rather well. You have my permission to make this letter public. Your most obliged,*

Palermo, 16th May 1927 (Anno V)

Dear Sirs,
As a consequence of energetic and reckless use, my noble testicles found themselves reduced to a sorry state. I had them removed and replaced with a pair supplied by you, *Valencia* model, which have enabled me to cut, in a few sylvan occasions, an excellent figure. Despite my bad habit of leaving them after use in a drawer full of live cockroaches, and dead coleoptera besides, exposed to the fumes of prussic acid, their state of preservation is exemplary, and a little Sidol restores their proper glossiness. Heartfelt thanks.*

Palermo, 2nd April 1925 (Anno IV)

Dear Sirs,
Being without testicles from the day of my birth, I had had recourse to the most celebrated firms and had tried all their devices, those applied from behind as well as those administered orally. In vain! But your *Excelsiors* saved me. I am a new man! Now I even experience a slight emotion, lasting 4 seconds, when I find myself in skin-to-skin contact with two naked eighteen-year-old girls. If I need testicles, I shall apply to you; and Italian music will be the richer.*

NOTES
Three sheets of lined paper, six sides.

p. 93, *Anno VI*: Year six of the Fascist era, calculated since the March on Rome (27th–29th October 1922). The dates are not entirely congruous.

p. 93, *mah-jongs*: See sixth note to p. 5.

p. 94, *decadent poets and Pizzetti-like musicians*: An allusion to Lucio Piccolo, poet and composer. "Pizzetti-like musicians" refers to Ildebrando Pizzetti, the composer from Parma noted for his melodic recitative.

p. 94, *all the riches of their palettes*: A joke directed at Casimiro, the painter.

p. 94, *entomological societies... acid-proof*: A joke on Raniero Alliata, the entomologist.

p. 95, *Eumolpus and Giton in bed*: The old poet Eumolpus and the handsome boy Giton of Petronius's *Satyricon*. In the novel, Giton is the lover of the student Encolpius, but Lampedusa's mistake could be an intentional jab at Lucio Piccolo.

p. 95, *Your most obliged*: The testimonial is initialled with a scribble. It is to be understood as signed by Casimiro Piccolo.

p. 96, *Heartfelt thanks*: Here the following scribble stands for the signature of Raniero Alliata.

p. 96, *will be the richer*: The apocryphal testimonial, once again initialled with a flourish, is attributed to Lucio Piccolo.

XVIII

I do not know, dear Casimiro, what critical approach you adopted when reading my last letter – I am certain, however, that it was erroneous. To deduce – from a momentary weakness, from a bout of sensual melancholy (which is the consequence of, and prelude to, bull-like erotic feats) – that I had gone completely *nuts* was a risky, fallacious and base hypothesis. I know, I know well enough, that some enfeeblement of the Monster's fibre would be received with great joy by the false friends, the false mystics and the veritable impostors who might hope to get along in peace, free from the harassment of the Monster's daily vigilance.

But there is a long way to go from the desire to its *Erfül-lung*.* And the Monster is lively, vigorous and equipped with 36 pairs of roaring balls.

Tomorrow the Monster is leaving for Siena. And on the 22nd he will be in Rome (Hôtel Quirinale), where he hopes to get your news and, perhaps, the precise details of your departure for C.d.O.* The Monster expects to arrive on 6th December.

Will we perhaps have H.S.H. the O.S.* as a plaintive tra-velling companion, and an absurd laughing stock during our coastal adventures?

The drowsy Monster
(9 o'clock in the morning)

99

NOTES

Only one sheet (two sides) of lined paper. The year is marked on a slant on the top-right corner of the recto. Below, it reads: "Florence", and below that: "18th November".

p. 99, *Erfüllung*: "Fulfilment" (German).
p. 99, *C.d.O.*: Capo d'Orlando, where Villa Piccolo is located.
p. 99, *H.S.H. the O.S.*: "His Serene Highness the Old Swine" (see note to p. 15), Prince of the Holy Roman Empire.

1928

XIX

Paris, 8th June 1928

The Monster, one hour before his departure for London…

You may imagine his state of mind if you compare it to the one you experienced so many times at Brindisi an hour before embarking for the Indies.

Paris is not too bad either. And this year, since I had the good sense to stop there on my way to London, it has made a great impression on me. Thinking back on that Etruscan hypogeum which is Palermo, it does not seem to me to be on the same planet. This year for the first time I searched for and found that fountain, which still exists in the Rue du Bac, in whose basin the venerable backside of the Abbé Jérôme rested for a long time while he read Boethius wearing spectacles with one broken lens and the other one missing.* In your name too I have shed an emotional tear.

In Henry, Chapelier, Rue Trenchat, I have seen an umbrella with a folding handle and tip, which means it can be carried in a suitcase. It costs 85 francs, that is 56 lire; and it is very fine –

The wandering Monster

Greetings to the Poet, if he is still alive.*

NOTES

Light blue card with the heading of the "Hôtel du Louvre / Paris".
Two sides.

p. 103, *Abbé Jérôme... missing*: The episode alluded to is in
Anatole France's novel *The Queen Pédauque*. See note to p. 68.

p. 103, *if he is still alive*: The postscript is added above the
heading of the hotel, on the right, within a box marked out by
pen and ink.

XX

London Scenes

I
The Vassal King

Just now the Monster's hotel is also accommodating a king. To be precise, H.H. Sofori Atta,* sovereign of an extensive but backward territory on the Ivory Coast. He is one of the many princelings whom "ruling Britannia" keeps chained to her steel trident and whom every now and then she is pleased to reward by inviting them to London so that they may admire the *buses*, the *chorus girls*, the artificial hares and other delightful Britannic specialities, begging them also not to forget the number and efficiency of the *tanks*, cruisers and bombers. But Sofori Atta, who appears to have distinguished himself in local guerrilla warfare against rebel tribes, is also here to receive the title of *knight*. Consequently we read in the papers the strange wording *H.M. Sir Sofori Atta*. "You who are kings in Sardinia and citizens in Pisa."* It is the first time he has been away from Africa, and he has told the newspapers that he is impressed by steam, and that trains frighten him, but that London struck him dumb. I imagine that is almost the same impression as anyone would get coming straight from Palermo.

This gentleman, black as a fountain pen and of a particularly ugly subspecies of Negro, is however most dignified, and he is besides the only sovereign who goes about always dressed as a king, with his fat limbs enveloped in a red velvet mantle with gold braid and lined with white fur (added, I hope, in homage to the English climate) and a fine crown on his head; but the ensemble is rather spoilt by his large yellow shoes and the large cigar which he has perpetually in his mouth.

The Monster often encounters him in the corridors accompanied by a little boy bearing (nonchalantly) a sceptre (of ivory, naturally). H.M. responds with great benevolence to the Monster's bows and smiles, exposing an incredible expanse of teeth (also of ivory), perhaps imagining (with Valéry) the "*future fumée*" of roast Monster.*

Tomorrow, they are taking the poor devil on a flight, and the following day he will go to Buckingham Palace and kneel before the King, who will dub him knight, like Galahad and Bayard*... But King George will soon be punished for such profanity, because he has to give him the kiss of peace.

II
A Cat

Two days ago the Monster was crossing Parliament Square, just by the side of the enormous Gothic edifice on which the London smoke and fog have managed in such a short time to confer such a venerable appearance, when from a kind of loophole adorned with the roses of Lancastra, the thistle of Scotland, and the shamrock of Erin* appeared a cat, a large cat as black as Sofori Atta, but much better-looking. With customary agility it came down a couple of metres of smooth wall, crossed the pavement and, with a rashness uncharacteristic of its race, made to cross the street. And that was in a place where there are no side roads and hence no *policemen* and no traffic islands, and where the motor cars, knowing that no one would ever venture across, speed along recklessly. It was marvellous to see the cat begin a kind of dance, a series of leaps, tumbles and somersaults, in an effort to avoid the darting vehicles. A dog would have been dispatched ten times over. After a couple of minutes of elegant acrobatics which made everyone pause on the pavement, it gave up. It took advantage of a few seconds' respite, came back, jumped onto the kerb, which it "had descended with such proud confidence",* and disappeared through the window among the carved roses, thistles and shamrocks – to lively applause from the bystanders. The Monster had never before seen a cat abandon its intention, and that filled him with intense delight.

III
Belinda and the Monster*

This evening there is a ball at the French Embassy. Madame l'Ambassadeur receives the guests at the top of the staircase. Tens of centuries have passed over her body, enveloped in a slim tunic the colour of *risotto alla Milanese*, and every one has left its mark there: the eighteenth century its powder, the nineteenth its anaemia, the twentieth the deformities brought about by ill-judged *sports* practised too late in life.

Below, the footman pounds out the names: "His Highness the Prince von Bismarck", a skinny little bespectacled shrimp, far removed from the bull-like power of his formidable grandfather; "the Count and the Countess von Blücher", "His Grace the Duke of Wellington"* – a momentous trio of names ironically brought together by Fate, one after the other, under this French roof. Diminished and subdued, the national disasters of France kiss bony pomp. His Excellency smiles behind his beard; he is desperately trying to find witticisms that are at the same time full of bonhomie, profundity and dignity; he invokes the protection of his master Talleyrand;* he cannot find it; he clears his throat.

In the ballroom, beneath the Georgian plasterwork, *jazz* music is raging. From the wall Louis XIV, the irreplaceable King of France, within the ermine and azure of his cloak, is careful not to smile. The Monster contemplates the *silver arms* of Belinda.

Later, with Belinda on his arm, he descends the stairway to go to supper; the crowds of the replete who are once more going up look in disdain at the descending crowds of the starving. Then, under the dim pinkish light of the *abat-jours*, the Monster is obliged to blend the contrasting delights of the cardinal-red lobsters and the sky-blue eyes of Belinda, while it would be very pleasant to relish them separately. Belinda, with delicious British candour, says silly things which her perfectly shaped mouth renders more precious than the wisdom of Buddha. The Monster tries not to get over-excited, but he does not succeed and, like His Excellency, he clears his throat. And by now the strawberries have all gone ("*comme le fruit se change en jouissance…*");* we have to leave; Belinda's short dress, with its descending heavy folds, rustles; up above, the music has struck up again. "*As in her silks my Coelia goes.*" Around Belinda the Corinnes, the Silvias, the Celias, the Rosalinds materialize, the *beautiful women* of Yeats, the evanescent apparitions of *Adonais*, the pallor of Rossetti's ladies, the fresh grace of Meredith's heroines – all the things that the Monster, incurably literary, can at that moment evoke.*

For some instants golden hair glimmers through the motor car's window.

The Monster is pining away.

He goes back to the hotel.

IV

Countryside

Dr Castellani (or rather Sir Aldo Castellani)* is driving his motor car. The Monster is sitting by him. Knightsbridge, Hammersmith, Putney, Kingston; kilometre after kilometre of a city which will not bring itself to an end. Suddenly, after Kingston, open fields. The narrow road winds between hawthorn hedges and huge trees. It goes up, it winds down without any apparent destination. Beyond the hedges undulating meadows, copses, red and white houses. Castellani, overcome with divine frenzy, steps on the accelerator: 30, 40, 50, 60, 70 *miles* per hour: the Rolls-Royce dashes obediently along without any vibrations or noise. The air becomes better and clearer. Then the hills of Surrey: ripples of earth which from their low altitudes reveal endless panoramas. "*Teas!*" "*Teas!*" "*Refreshments!*" "*Petrol!*" "*Tyres*" announce the signs on the buildings along the road. Guildford presents its one old, straight, downhill Elizabethan street. Afterwards, new hills, and the woodland.

Through the leaves the sun shines onto the street in golden scales; the wet fields are scented, as ever, by recently fallen rain; the sky is striving to resemble a Turner, often with success. In the distance, magnificent vertical clouds, grazing the brows of the hills, are coloured slantwise in smoky amber. The Monster would like to have Belinda by his side instead of this most learned and excellent man – Belinda, so much less learned, so much more precious.

The wood grows denser, but there, in a clearing, is a house surrounded by rhododendrons. The fire is lit in the drawing room: it drives away the damp, and it would drive away melancholy too if the blue base of the flickering flames did not look so much like Belinda's eyes. The garden behind stretches out into vast grassland, chequered with the ruby sand of the *tennis* courts. Tea is served. *Enter* mother and daughter. The Doctor talks heartily about trichinosis, and describes its horrible symptoms; he denies that it is a purely tropical disease; he declares that the bacilli can be found in any intestines. The Monster, beneath those expert eyes, trembles and recalls those of Sofori Atta: one wants the Monster's cutlets in order to eat them, the other his entrails to study them. Ah! Belinda, on the other hand, wants nothing from the Monster! But this is bad too.

I am on the way back. It is evening. By the roadside, overturned cars and smashed motorcycles: the wreckage of the weekend break. Just beyond the edge of the wood, there are tents, or even simple rugs, under which or on which holidaying couples take tea or something else. Streets like roller coasters. The Doctor asks the Monster the history of Napoleon, and when they get to Austerlitz he runs over a hen. Shouts, complaints: the blood money is fixed at 5 shillings.

In the distance the aurora borealis appears: it is London. The Evil Beast spreads out its tentacles: the countryside asserts itself for one last time. Here we are. Here are the *policemen*. It is a quarter to eight: the Monster must dress for dinner.

He goes back to the hotel.

V
Technicalities

A mass of leather armchairs from the ceiling almost down to the floor in the cinema. The walls around decorated with that particular smooth matt gold, lightly adorned with coloured flowers, which seems to be the (by no means despicable) modern architectural trend. The *foyer* is very beautiful: the walls are alternate strips of steel and copper, like propeller blades. This Paramount in London is exactly like the one in Paris: both of them boast of being the most *up to date* in the world. And then there is Movietone* – and I do not understand why they do not speak more about this, since it provides the answer to cinematography with speech. This is the only way *films* are produced from real life. And the military reviews with their music in motion, the rhythm of the steps, the roar of the cannon, the sound of the commands and the applause of the crowd are rendered quite perfectly. Likewise the sporting *matches* with the howling of the masses, the launching of ships with hammer blows, the rustle of the keels, the splashing water, the sirens and the applause; and various opening speeches, not only with a perfect synchronization of the motion of the lips and the sound, but also with noises in the distance, the voices of the crowd and the horns of motor cars and the drone of aeroplanes. But the most beautiful of all is a scene on the Welsh coast in which the throbbing of the sea, the crashing of the foam, the whistle of the wind and the cries of innumerable seagulls were rendered admirably. It is of course a system for the simultaneous recording of sounds and pictures on one machine.

Afterwards, a garden was shown. In the background a hedge; an old gentleman with a white beard came out of it and drew near: you could hear the gravel crunching under his feet. When he reached the foreground, he stopped and gave a brief speech: it was Shaw.* The clarity of the words, without a trace of phonographic creaking, the complete and perfect synchronization (any defects would have been noticed, given that the whole immense screen was occupied by the subject's head and shoulders) were really amazing.

Next week we shall hear Cestertonio,* even though the papers maliciously say that the whole screen will not be big enough for his opulent figure.

I think that you, with your craze for light-hearted *films*, are cut off from all the progress in cinematography. I have seen one called *The Crowd*,* which is certainly sad, but truly beautiful: the cruel atmosphere of big cities is captured with great vigour. Besides, I believe that the Pittalugas* are effecting a kind of castration on the films which they allow to enter Italy: the critics in the newspapers here do nothing but mention and praise boldly conceived German or American *films* of the fantasy and realistic genres, which in Italy we have had no wind of. Anyhow, all the *films* on view here are always bolder and less *milk and water* than those which Pittaluga presents.

* * *

The Monster does not know whether you are in the country or not. But he is sending this to Palermo.

I should like to have your news.

And regards from

The Metropolitan Monster.

NOTES

On paper headed "Hôtel Great Central, London, N.W. 1". Ten numbered sheets, twenty sides.

p. 105, *H.H. Sofori Atta*: A reference to Nana Sir Ofori Atta, King of Akyem Abuakwa, one of the largest and wealthiest kingdoms of the then Gold Coast Colony.

p. 105, *You who are kings... Pisa*: A quotation from Giosuè Carducci's poem 'Local Feud', in *New Verses* (LXXIX).

p. 106, *"future fumée" of roast Monster*: "Future fumée" is a quotation from Paul Valéry's poem 'The Graveyard by the Sea', in *Charmes*: "*je hume ici ma future fumée*" ("here I breathe the smoke of my future").

p. 106, *like Galahad and Bayard*: Like the knight of the Round Table, Galahad, and like Pierre du Terrail, "Seigneur de Bayard". But Bayard is also Rinaldo's magic horse in Ariosto's *Orlando Furioso*. This may explain the malicious ellipsis in the letter.

p. 107, *Lancastra... Erin*: Lancastra is the Latin name of Lancaster. Erin (originally Erínn) is the ancient and poetic name of Ireland.

p. 107, *had descended with such proud confidence*: A quotation from General Armando Diaz's Victory Address of 4th November 1918, in which he communicated the rout of the Austrian army and the victory of the Italians in the war.

p. 107, *Belinda and the Monster*: A reference to *La Belle et la Bête*, seventeenth-century fairy story by Madame Leprince de Beaumont, entitled in Italian *Belinda e il Mostro* (*Belinda and the Monster*). Hence, Belinda and Lampedusa, where Belinda is at the same time the adorable Rosalind of *As You Like It*. See also sixth note to p. 6.

113

p. 108, *Bismarck... Blücher... Wellington*: Prince von Bismarck's "formidable grandfather" was Otto von Bismarck, a dominant figure in late nineteenth-century world affairs. Gebhart Leberecht von Blücher, Count Blücher's ancestor, had been a Prussian general at the time of the Napoleonic wars. Arthur Wellesley, grandfather of the Duke of Wellington attending the French Embassy ball, was in command of the forces which defeated Napoleon at Waterloo in June 1815.

p. 108, Talleyrand: A reference to the French diplomat Charles Maurice de Talleyrand-Périgord.

p. 108, *comme le fruit se change en jouissance*: An adapted quote from Paul Valéry's 'The Graveyard by the Sea': "*Comme le fruit se fond en jouissance*" ("Even as a fruit melts into pleasure").

p. 109. *As in her silks... evoke*: "As in her silks my Coelia goes" is a quote from Robert Herrick's poem 'Upon Julia's Clothes', altough in Herrick's line the woman's name is Julia. Corinne is the protagonist of Madame de Staël's *Corinne, or Italy*. Sylvia is a character in Shakespeare's *The Two Gentlemen of Verona*. Celia and Rosalind are characters in *As You Like It*. Yeats is the Irish poet W.B. Yeats. "*Adonais*" is probably a reference to Percy Bysshe Shelley's elegy on the death of John Keats. Rossetti and Meredith are references to Dante Gabriel Rossetti and George Meredith respectively.

p. 109, *Sir Aldo Castellani*: Aldo Castellani was one of the greatest authorities of the time on tropical diseases. He held professorships in London and Naples. He was also the doctor for Roman high society and the Lanza family.

p. 111, *Movietone*: A system for registering and synchronizing pictures and words on optical tape, invented by Freeman Harrison Owens in 1924. The patent was acquired by Fox Film Co. in 1926.

p. 112, *Shaw*: George Bernard Shaw.

p. *Cestertonio*: See note to p. 67.

p. 112, *The Crowd*: A celebrated film by King Vidor (1928). It portrays a troubled America on the eve of the economic crisis.

p. 112, *the Pittalugas*: The Società Anonima Stefano Pittaluga, founded in 1925, became the largest firm of cinematographic distributors, owning more than two hundred and fifty cinemas.

XXI

The Monster has written, as often from Paris as from here, various letters, all of which reveal in their content the customary sagacity of his spirit, while in their form they sparkle with every venusty of style.

To not a single one of these has the Monster received a reply. The Monster was so angered by this that some days ago he tore up some precious pages ready to be sent, in which very important occurrences of London life were described in a lively manner and acutely analysed: the dog races, the talking *films*, the dinners at Paletto's,* the Monster's popularity, together with profound contemplations on the English constitution, the situation in Egypt and the new safety razors. A literary treasure trove now irremediably lost in a fit of righteous anger.

Now, having come to a calmer consideration of the matter, and thinking that this persistent silence was perhaps the result of the Sicilian dog days which must have dried up even the bottles of ink now that all watercourses are gone, he is sending this, which has the form and force of an *ultimatum*.

In about ten days the Monster is leaving England. He will go to Holland, from there to Germany and, via

Cologne, Mainz, Bonn, Frankfurt, Worms, Speyer, Coblenz, Wiesbaden, Strasbourg, Basle and Zurich, he will reach his mother at Innsbruck.

There is no need to tell you what you will lose if the Monster decides to be silent. He will certainly do so if he does not receive your news before he leaves London.

His observations on the Rembrandts of The Hague and the Vermeers of Amsterdam, the porcelains of Delft and the tulips of Harlem, on the birthplace of Goethe,* the Emperors of Worms, German Gothic, the legendary Rhine, the philosophical Basle and the august Cologne – things which would have been part of your intellectual patrimony – will be lost to you.

And so, with threats, greetings from –

The obdurate Monster

NOTES

On paper headed "Hôtel Great Central, London, N.W. 1". Three numbered sheets, six sides.

p. 115, *Paletto's*: See fourth note to p. 65.
p. 116, *the birthplace of Goethe*: Frankfurt.

XXII

The Monster's wrath is slightly lessened by the reception of your letter, which came yesterday. It turns out to be all the more welcome to him since it arrived before the expiration of his *ultimatum* – an indication of spontaneous contrition which is highly valued by the Monster.

The letter, sprinkled with very fine salt,* has once again confirmed the Monster's opinion of the equal ability with which the King of Poland* wields the pen and the brush; a versatility which is however exceeded by Lucio, whose paintings are without doubt superior to his verses, since they enjoy the incomparable merit of invisibility, a merit not always shared by his poems and his music.

That said, the Monster must state how surprised and saddened he was by the wretched pedantry and the falsity of the witticisms directed at him in the dispute over the moon.

He has definitely seen this moon, and the objections he makes to the opposing line of argument are of two kinds: one practical, one scientific. Above all, considering its length, that letter cannot have been composed in one day, and it could well be that the almanac indicates a new moon on the 13th, while the Monster observed that satellite on the 10th or the 9th or the 15th.

Secondly, although Piana* is the centre of the universe, and the stars have been created expressly to rotate about it in immutable order, one has nevertheless to take into consideration a series of astronomical phenomena which mean that the lunar months are not equal in all countries. For this purpose, you must bear in mind the existence of tidal charts showing noticeable variations between points on the same coast, which are infinitely less distant from each other than the olive-rich hillsides of Capo d'Orlando and the busy banks of the Thames.

Anyhow, the phenomenon of a special moon for London, even if it were true, would not be as wonderful as that mentioned in one part of your letter: "I use English hair pomade". The fact that English hairs grow on the hide of a native of Palermo is surprising and the Monster, to avoid such feelings in future, suggests that you learn grammar and write in future: "I use English pomade for my hair".

* * *

Fulco has been here for two days only, invited specially to take part in a dinner given by Lady Wimborne in honour of the King of Spain – which casts some shadows, hopefully unfounded, on this most noble Monarch. The Monster did not have the good fortune to see him, but he has once or twice met Lady Wimborne, about whom he has heard things which are absolutely impossible to put into writing and which would make even the Old Swine's backside blush.*

* * *

For ten days we have had uninterrupted good weather here. The sun shines for sixteen hours a day, and London has changed its usual subtle chromatic harmonies of greens darkening into browns and of browns shading off through all gradations of grey into silver for the blinding light and the velvety shadows of a Spanish city. Of course many fine Englishmen are dying, whether from the heat or from surprise is not known. The newspapers publish accounts of the state of health of the animals in the zoo, and it appears that the lions and the tigers are badly affected by the heat while the polar bears are fine. A mandrill has died. It looks as though Cirino needed a soul in exchange.*

A *policeman* was left stuck by his feet to the roadway asphalt as it softened in the heat. And he was roaring, but he had to wait for his boots to be taken off before he could walk. He was mercilessly photographed.

Of his worldly pleasures the Monster will say nothing. He gave a full description of them on a sheet which he then destroyed. His popularity knows no bounds.

* * *

The Monster has received from the Old Swine a sumptuously illustrated letter; it appears that he has given himself over to a kind of positivist and scientific coenobitism in the woods of Ficuzza – which must conceal an abyss of perversion.

The Monster is leaving London at the beginning of August on the itinerary which he has mentioned.

The Monster says goodbye because he is tired. It is 3 in the afternoon; the heat is great, as it would be even for Palermo. Besides, the Monster has just returned from a rather too tasty lunch at Claridge's, to which he paid rather too much honour. And a light siesta with a volume of Belloc* and a jug of iced water would be not unwelcome.

The placated Monster

Please admire the handwriting: a lapis-lazuli Parker Duofold Senior Pen.

NOTES
On paper headed "Hôtel Great Central, London, N.W. 1". Four numbered sheets, eight sides.

p. 117, *sprinkled with very fine salt*: See first note to p. 43.

p. 117, *the King of Poland*: A reference to Casimiro Piccolo, who shared his first name with the most famous king in Polish history, Casimir III.

p. 118, *Piana*: The district in which Villa Piccolo is located.

p. 118, *Fulco... Lady Wimbourne... King of Spain... Old Swine's backside blush*: For Fulco, see first note to p. 46. Alice Wimborne, wife of Ivor Guest, 1st Viscount Wimborne, and later lover of the composer William Walton. The King of Spain at the time was Alfonso XIII. For "Old Swine", see note to p. 15.

p. 119, *Cirino needed a soul in exchange*: The reference to Cirino has not been identified, although it could be another nickname for the monkey-like Mah-Jong. See note to p. 15.

p. 120, *Belloc*: A reference to the Anglo-French poet, historian and Catholic apologist Hilaire Belloc.

XXIII

[Paris, August 1928]

Like the newborn babe snatched from his mother's womb, with the same shrieks and tears and blood which scorches no less for being metaphorical, just so the Monster left the honey-sweet hive of his mother London. Tatters of his heart remain hanging from the trees by every house in the delightful city, and the Channel, temptingly calm, has been crossed by a petrified Monster. But Picardy – where the dwarf pines fight off the menace of the sand – and the stonework at Amiens, and the sculptured vine shoot which runs along the entire cornice of the famous nave, and the bronze tombs of the young bishops of the 12th century – where the holy prelates sleep sustained by lion-like Faith and indifferent to the dirty wicked beasts (as they were depicted by the ardent spirit of the unknown artist) – and the delicacy of some duck pies not shy of truffles, and the peaceful buoyancy of the French soul – all availed, certainly not to suffocate the grief, but to spread upon it a patina of new memories which alone gives life to impassioned spirits (such as the Monster).

So it was in more restrained torment that the Monster was able to cross Île-de-France, golden with crops in the hollows, and green at the crests of the woods in such a way that the light, better reflected where it is less abundant, invests it with a steady, diffused silvery glow, of a mildness and charm truly incomparable.

At Chantilly the Monster stopped and saw parks and castles and ancient furniture to make Masnata* feel the chill of death, and legendary diamonds and illustrious ambers. It is in this solitary, almost rustic residence that the thoughtful traveller is best able to appreciate the rich treasure of elegant energy which the great Kings brought to France, and in the atrocious scars of war, which are present everywhere, the indomitable fervour of this valiant race.

The Monster's window overlooks Rue de Lille, one of the most aristocratic streets in this aristocratic *faubourg*. Opposite there is a building, an *hôtel particulier** (which certainly does not mean a hostelry, as I am sure you know), which is exactly how the Monster always imagined the Hôtel de Guermantes,* with its long narrow windows adorned above with baroque shells and below with wrought-iron railings, with its small well-proportioned courtyard separated from the street by the wall surmounted by balusters. The Monster expects any moment to see Charlus's paunch appear at the end of the street intently following *une petite télégraphiste* or visiting Jupien,* for even here wretched little shops stand side by side with luxurious mansions.

O gentle beauty of provincial Paris – of quiet streets, of decorative façades, of loquacious, sharp-witted gossips, of ingenious shops! – beauty ignored by so many people, who mistake the soiled cosmopolitan mask of Montmartre for the true aspect of this affable city, as calm and modestly industrious as any other. This is a side which all the great artists have been able to recognize and express, such as the

Monster, Anatole France, Rilke (*Aufzeichnungen*),* and so many pages of Proust – but one which will always remain unknown to sterile super-aesthetes (Lucio) and spineless sensual monsters (Pitruzzo).*

And so we go on.

And you, what are you doing? What chimerical dreams of fame is Lucio chasing? (Fame understood as something that may be won without any contribution from genius, work or chance.)

What emasculated illustrations is Casimiro working on?

And are you still in the country, leaning to catch the messages of the wind, to hear the song of Aeolian Sirens – or has the gigantic tumult and swirl of the city captured you again?

The Monster (who is known here simply as "Monsieur G. Tomasi") is still at the Hôtel du Louvre – Place du Théâtre Français. For he is staying here only temporarily, and tomorrow perhaps he will leave his beautiful room and his aristocratic view.

And the Monster will always be glad to get your news –

The solitary Monster

NOTES

On paper headed "Hotel Palais D'Orsay". Two double sheets of graph paper (numbered 1 and 2), eight sides.

p. 122, *Masnata*: See first note to p. 6.
p. 122, *hôtel particulier*: A private mansion (French).
p. 122, *Hôtel de Guermantes*: The Duchess de Guermantes's residence in Marcel Proust's *In Search of Lost Time*.
p. 122, *Charlus's paunch… Jupien*: Charlus is the "pot-bellied" Palamède de Guermantes, Baron de Charlus of Proust's *In Search of Lost Time*. "*Une petite télégraphiste*" is French for

"a little telegraphist". Jupien, a former waistcoat-maker, is Charlus's male lover.

p. 123, *Aufzeichnungen*: A reference to Rainer Maria Rilke's novel *Die Aufzeichnungen des Malte Laurids Brigge* ("*The Notebooks of Malte Laurids Brigge*").

p. 123, *Pitruzzo*: See note to p. 15.

XXIV

Zurich (date as postmarked)

The Monster has been away from Switzerland for fifteen years. No short time in the life of a mortal, especially if you consider that then the Monster was in the first (but promising) flourish of his youth, while now he finds himself in all the vigour of his manhood; and if you consider what a mass of events has occurred since then throughout European society, and what a throng of personal experiences have amassed since then on the Monster's head, making him white at the temples, reducing his heart to the state of an extinguished ember, but enriching his intelligence with a sensibility and a culture not merely rare but unique – (so it is, and it is blasphemy to doubt it) –

The principal result of a journey to Switzerland is that one travels in time more than in space. One lives in pre-war Europe, in the easy-going Europe of 1913. The bread is white, soft, delicate and golden-brown… as it used to be; cigarettes cost 35 cents for ten… what they used to cost; when dinner is over (a Monster dinner, you understand) the bill comes to 4.30, and if one leaves a tip to make it up to 5, one is considered a nabob; a tram ride is 15 cents, marvellous; and the huge, rich, excellent pastries cost the same; and if the Monster wishes to delight his spirit, he pays 2.25 for a Tauchnitz* and 2 lire for a seat (the best) in a cinema. These figures are of course somewhat deceptive, because the exchange rate is pretty steep and brings you down to earth; but there is always a certain margin of profit – and besides the Monster is not preoccupied with sordid financial matters but with psychological games and repercussions.

Here in the architecture on the street the newest German – or rather Assyrian – style flourishes. And the most paltry bank has the grandeur of the palace in Ecbatana.* That is preferable to the little varnished papier-mâché houses with which the Palermitan firms play around, and they give the city a *cossu** appearance which is not to be despised; all the same the "family chapel" style to which these architects evidently aspire ends up being somewhat depressing.

The Monster hangs about these sedate streets and admires the police officers directing the traffic from the height of their unnecessary raised platforms (oh, who will be equal to the task of singing the classic simplicity of Him, of the more than human London *policeman* who, if you ask him the way, does not bend down or bat an eyelid but lets fall, from the top of Mont Blanc, towards you, poor little mouse, a *"First right, second left"* and withdraws into a persistent but not hostile silence which nothing could disturb again, while you writhe at the level of his belt buckle?) or the innumerable boxes hung on the lights for the various kinds of refuse, or the white-and-blue trams smelling of turpentine, or the bookshops full of Insel Verlag volumes, which one of these days may drive the Monster to steal!

But there are also the old streets, with *Erkern** and conical roofs, with steep flights of steps and bright-blue canals (all clean, for it is a Palermitan error to believe that the picturesque is inseparable from filth). Over these streets hovers the slightly uncheerful shade of Zwingli, that fiery reformer who worked out a more desperately predestinarian theology than that of Calvin, towards which Revel* (who has the best of reasons to wish for a God of infinite mercy) has vowed unyielding hatred.

The Monster cannot provide information on culinary specialties: although the cuisine is generally excellent, it lacks any particular character, and the genius of the Swiss has never risen to those sublime gastronomical concepts which are the immortal glory of Italy, France and (in their own way) of Germany too. As with everything that is in force here, so with the cuisine there is an enlightened good sense which does not however permit the sublime paradoxes of "pasta with sardines" and "*caneton rouennais*",* wonderful triumphs of irrationality against the cold dictates of logic.

The day after tomorrow the Monster is going to Innsbruck, where he will meet his mother, your aunt. And since you have not deigned to write, he too will stay silent – and so you will miss out on the rest of these instructive and delightful lectures, and you will miss out on the reports on post-war Austria, on Bavarian cuisine, on how the Monster and his Mother are thrashed by the Tyrolean mob and other delightful and humorous events. And that will make you bite your nails –

The Alpine Monster –

(who can be contacted: Postlagernd – Innsbruck – Austria).

PS: Being at a loose end in Basle the other evening, the Monster let himself be persuaded by a cinematographic *réclame* to go and see a *film* starring Norma Shearer.*

A charming creature!

The *film* itself was a bit silly; even though, with elephantine grace, the programme describes it as *"Ein Lustspiel voller Champagnerlaune"*.*

* * *

Lucio need have no fear: his *Weisse Haus** has been looked after and will be returned to him.

* * *

Tomorrow the Monster is going to the picture gallery: it is full of paintings by Hodler,* who was from Zurich and left everything to the city.

* * *

In the hotel there is a young lady who looks exactly like Fulco* – that is, she is not beautiful. All the same she is pleasant. At the moment she is sitting near the Monster and laughs precisely as that illustrious man does.

* * *

My respectful regards to O.S.,* if he has not yet been eaten up by resuscitated cockroaches. He knows that I have the highest esteem for him, and if he reads these lines I beg him to look after the two volumes of Proust which *are in his* possession.

NOTES

On paper headed "Hotel Habis-Royal" of Zurich. Two numbered sheets, four sides. The letter is of September 1928.

p. 126, *Tauchnitz*: A series of English narratives, called "Library of British and American Authors", was started in Leipzig in 1841 by Christian Bernhard Freiherr von Tauchnitz. Its worldwide distribution was very effective in spreading the English language.

p. 126, *Ecbatana*: A reference to the ancient Persian and later Parthian city of Ecbatana, situated at the foot of Mount Alvand.

p. 126, *cossu*: "Opulent" (French).

p. 126, *does not bend down*: In this passage Lampedusa jokingly alludes to Dante's meeting with the haughty spirit of Farinata degli Uberti in *Inferno* (x, 73–75).

p. 126, *Erkern*: Projecting balconies, in masonry, with windows.

p. 127, Revel: See first note to p. 83.

p. 127, *caneton rouennais*: Duckling à la Rouen.

p. 127, Norma Shearer: One of the most popular actresses at the time. In 1928 she was twenty-six.

p. 128, *Ein Lustspiel voller Champagnerlaune*: "A comedy full of festive spirit" (German).

p. 128, *Weisse Haus*: *Das weisse Haus* (*"The White House"*), a novel by the Danish writer Herman Bang.

p. 128, *Hodler*: The landscape painter Ferdinand Hodler.

p. 128, *Fulco*: See first note to p. 46.

p. 128, O.S.: See note to p. 15.

1929

XXV

[Rome,] 17th May [1929]

The Monster finished his journey in material comfort (we found a carriage that was almost empty), but troubled with unhappy thoughts. In a nearby compartment there was a young lady who bore in her hair and her nose some slight signs of the divine Rosalind* – of whom she was, in fact, a fellow citizen. This was enough to make her acceptable to the heart of the Monster, who later managed to establish that the resemblance to Rosalind was purely superficial, because this beautiful girl was really *une cochonne*, in the words of the Duchess of Guermantes.*

Today was my interview here with young Alice and her consort:* they have played an important and noble role in our troubles, and have decided to break off all relations with the criminal couple,* who even with them have been lavish with insults and abuse and, as is their wont, the very day after receiving financial help!

* * *

Yesterday I was in the Senate, sitting in the gallery, for Castellani's* swearing-in. He advanced, preceded by two ushers and followed by two escorts, in a somewhat lugubrious procession! He looked like a condemned man being led to the scaffold, and instead he was ascending to supreme beatitude, because he has derived from this nomination endless childlike joy. Since he has got it into his head that he owes the nomination to me, he showers me with thanks, which I accept with courteous composure. He has already been sounded out about his examination of Lucio: of his own accord he suggested using his name on the medical certificate (I hope that has already been done), and in London he will provide us with a life certificate, which he says will last for ever.

* * *

The Senate is very "Louis Philippe" in style. The hall, covered in inlaid wood, is dignified and spotless: it constitutes the most interesting and well-kept archaeological museum in Rome. From all the Senators, I think no more than 1,000 hairs could be gathered, but on the other hand there is a veritable forest of crutches and a mountain of surgical trusses. Altogether, the impression is of a "super-Bellini",* one even more sought after as the members are paid instead of paying. The voting urns are exact replicas of the famous ones in that distinguished place, down to the incomprehensibly subtle and *pompadour* colouring.

The Duce was there, yellow as a lemon. Read, if you can get hold of it (*Corriere d'Italia*, *Osservatore Romano*,* of the 16th), the violent speech of the Pope; truly noteworthy, particularly towards the end. They've already come to blows!* Please write to me and give me news of you and of Lucio's affairs –

Affectionately

The Monster

134

NOTES

On paper headed "Hotel Quirinal / Rome". Two sheets, four sides.

p. 133, *Rosalind*: See sixth note to p. 6.

p. 133, *une cochonne... the Duchess of Guermantes*: "A slut" (French). The Duchess of Guermantes is a character in Proust's *In Search of Lost Time*. See also Letter XXIII.

p. 133, *young Alice and her consort*: For "young Alice", see third note to p. 6.

p. 133, *the criminal couple*: Francesco Tomasi di Lampedusa (Uncle Ciccio) – Giuseppe's uncle and brother of Pietro Tomasi della Torretta – and his wife Angela Santucci. Angela, a fiery character from Romagna, had of old started a lawsuit against her brother-in-law, Prince Giulio, father of Giuseppe, involving inheritance. Giuseppe remembered a carpet stained with ink in a drawing room in the Palazzo Lampedusa, the result of an inkwell being thrown from a window in the upper storey, where Uncle Francesco and Aunt Angela were living. Relations between the couple and Giuseppe were to be again rather good after the Second World War.

p. 133, *Castellani's*: For Castellani, see second note to p. 109.

p. 134, *super-Bellini*: For the "Bellini", see third note to p. 5.

p. 134, *Corriere d'Italia, Osservatore Romano*: The name of two Italian dailies, the latter being the official newspaper of the Holy See.

p. 134, *They've already come to blows*: The Concordat between the Kingdom of Italy and the Holy See had been signed on 11th February 1929, but by May relations between Pius XI and Mussolini were again tense.

XXVI

[Rome,] 18th May [1929]

Dear Casimiro,

From a letter of Papa's received yesterday, I learn that you are always at his side in these grievous *démarches*,* and for that I am very grateful to you.

But I wish you could convince him and the lawyer and everyone else that there must be a warning, a report from police headquarters, in short a *document*, of all the criminal couple* have done; because otherwise there will be nothing but futile reprimands and warnings. Whereas with a police report and caution their position becomes precarious in the future.

You can tell Papa that my Uncle Torretta* is also of this opinion, because he is convinced, and does nothing but insist energetically, that there must be a report from police headquarters.

Affectionately

The Monster

NOTES

On paper headed "Hotel Quirinal / Rome". A single sheet, two sides.

p. 137, *démarches*: "Proceedings" (French).
p. 137, *the criminal couple*: See fourth note to p. 133.
p. 137, *Uncle Torretta*: The marchese della Torretta, Ambassador to London from 1922 to 1927.

1930

XXVII

My dearest Aunt,
On returning to Berlin I am hastening to give you the news, particularly about my stay in Livonia.

I have spent two weeks here, which have been so interesting and pleasant that I do not remember anything like them for a long while. I'm not talking about the affection and cordiality of my hosts, which would be enough to make a stay even in the least attractive of countries pleasing, but of the country itself, the woodland, the lakes, the mighty rivers, the sense of *coudées franches** which one has in those enormous, almost desert spaces, unlike this old Europe in which one is always crushed as on an overcrowded bus.

Of course I do not have to tell you how beautiful Stomersee is, with its immense *pelouses,** the lovely trees, the charming slope in the park towards the lake. And the immense avenues which stretch into the countryside. All this has not suffered at all, or at least I cannot imagine how it could be more beautiful than it is; everything has been well kept and very well looked after, and Stomersee is for many many kilometres around the only *Gutshaus** which has been restored to its ancient dignity, or at least maintained with the degree of elegance that befits it – which is for Licy* a source of great and justified pride.

In the house itself great changes have of course taken place since the last time you were here, and since I do not know the former *arrangement*, it will be hard for me to explain them to you. The *hall* at any rate is intact; by what seems to be a real miracle, neither the staircase nor the wood panelling was damaged. And it is this hall, to be precise an *encoignure** to the left when you enter, that is lived in.

On the left (entering the *hall*) there is a drawing room with fine antique furniture and bookshelves. From here one goes into a round study which occupies the bulging space of a tower. Then from the first drawing room one passes into what was the music room and which is now the dining room, with its four windows giving onto the garden, and its delicate Empire plasterwork. This is a truly impressive room of great elegance. Further on, what used to be the dining room and another sitting room have been left in their original state of devastation so that "memory of the deed might not fade yet".* Above, on the right at the top of the stairs, are Licy's and André's rooms (I have seen Licy's study with its fine Louis XVI furniture, her psychoanalysis library and the portrait of Freud); then on the left are the guest rooms.

We have had several outings: to Marienburg, with its beautiful park on the island in the lake; a lunch on the side of yet another lake, not far from the village of Stomersee, and where apparently Uncle too has been on an outing; and then we tried to go to Pechory, in Estonia, to see the Russian monastery, but we did not succeed in crossing the frontier because the car did not have the "triple document",* and after several vicissitudes we returned in the evening to Stomersee, having gone across half of Latvia, very interesting for me. We thought a lot about you, Uncle and Lolette,* and we were sorry you were not there too. The journey is very comfortable:

you leave Berlin at 9.30. The following day at 7 you arrive at Riga without any changes or difficulties of any kind – the wagons-lits and the *restaurants* are excellent.

I have two packets of Russian tea for you and two for Lolette, sent by Licy; I also had some Russian cigarettes for Uncle, but at the frontier the Germans demanded 50 marks to take them in! The cigarettes cost 40! I preferred to leave them. Uncle will pardon me and understand. I leave tomorrow for Dresden, where I shall have news of Mama. Continue to write to Palermo. Friendly greetings to Lolette and Biancheri. Love to you and Uncle

Giuseppe

NOTES

On paper headed "Koburger Hof-Berlin N.W.". Two numbered sheets, four sides. This letter does not belong to the Fondazione Biblioteca di via Senato's collection, but is part of the Lampedusa correspondence held by his heirs.

p. 141, *My dearest Aunt*: The aunt is Alice Barbi, widow of Baron Boris Wolff and wife of Lampedusa's uncle, Pietro Tomasi della Torretta. See third note to p. 6. Alice had not seen the castle of Stomersee, described here, since 1917.

p. 141, *coudées franches*: "Complete liberty" (French).

p. 141, *pelouses*: "Lawns" (French).

p. 141, *Gutshaus*: The residence on an estate.

p. 141, *Licy*: Alessandra Wolff Stomersee, called affectionately "Licy", future wife of Lampedusa and Alice Barbi's daughter (from her first marriage). Giuseppe and Licy became acquainted in 1925 in London, where they were both guests at the Italian Embassy, at that time in the charge of Alice Barbi's second husband, Pietro Tomasi della Torretta, Giuseppe's uncle. From the correspondence between the two it is evident that Lampedusa began to press her to marry him only in 1931.

p. 142, *encoignure*: "Corner" (French).

p. 142, *memory of the deed might not fade yet*: A quotation from Torquato Tasso (either from his 'On the Death of Ercole Gonzaga', *Rime*, 517, or from *Jerusalem Conquered* XII, 75), who was in turn quoting a poem by Petrarch (*Canzoniere* CXXVIII).

p. 142, *Licy's and André's rooms*: André Pilar, a Baltic baron of Spanish origin, was married at the time of the letter to Alessandra Wolff.

p. 142, *Pechory... triple document*: A reference to the famous Russian monastery of Pskovo-Pechorsky near the town of Pechory. The "triple document" was a customs document made up of three detachable parts.

p. 142, *Lolette*: Olga Wolff Stomersee, Licy's younger sister, who was married to the diplomat Augusto Biancheri.

XXVIII

[Berlin,] 13th August 1930

Just as the Monster, having slept soundly at last, was coming downstairs in order to go and entertain his stomach with some light refreshment, he was handed your letter. So it was that his delighted reading of it took place to the delightful accompaniment of rolls of different shapes and consistency, of jams made from various fruits, and of milk which this provident municipality manages to convey to the consumer not entirely skimmed.

The Monster saw with pleasure how the few radio-engineering magazines which came with it teemed with good news, and the marvels of the new HF light* made even his hardened heart miss a beat. But he does think that you sold such precious items too cheaply to Mormino,* and he hopes that any future inventions will be better rewarded.

The Monster will start collecting magazines and pamphlets once again, and he will make the enquiries you ask for; he does fear however that his German – which is, as everyone knows, of the purest kind, and has been learned in the good school of Goethe and Kleist, and which during these last weeks has been enriched with slang words, getting to the stage of making *calembours** in private conversations (to the amazement of the Baltic baroness who has inherited from her famous mother,* in a more refined way, a lack of belief in other people's knowledge) – will nevertheless not be up to an exchange of scientific ideas.

It is a pity that the Monster will not be here on the 22nd for the opening of the Radio Exhibition, for there would have been a very abundant harvest there.*

After the very pleasant week spent in Livonia, Berlin exerts once more its weird fascination on the cosmopolitan Monster. On the other hand, those large, almost empty lands, those shadowy, scented forests, the boundless horizons of grassy plains, the blue, rapid and inexhaustible rivers – all leave an enormous sense of nostalgia, while in this old, super-civilized Europe one always feels rather crushed as on an overcrowded bus. The creation of such a sense of nostalgia does owe something, however, to Riga's unbelievable confectionery shops and certain Russian delicacies made of duck, celery and puff pastry, which were as great a revelation for the Monster's tummy as Dostoevsky was for his spirit. This wonder is called *kulebyaka*, and I would be grateful if you could restrain yourself from making obscene jokes on the name,* since it is something worthy of the greatest respect.

His kind-of-Russian visit has, however, not been exclusively gastronomical: during this week the Monster has mastered some noble and very useful arts – typewriting and dancing – demonstrating for both an unexpected aptitude, and he has laid the foundations of an understanding of the Russian tongue which he intends to develop with private study.

Your close examination of the character of Vathek* is interesting and precise, and it is quite worthy of your penetrating mind, which is now known to everyone: it is true that the tragic element in the book only concerns the mother (and even in this it is not without its touches of the grotesque: remember the meal with the ghouls in the cemetery); we must not forget that Beckford is, basically, an eighteenth-century writer, and that therefore he regards all that with overarching irony.

The other day, when I was passing through Kovno,* the station was packed with Jewish members of the lower orders who had come to celebrate a fellow countryman who was going back to America. The spectacle was grotesque to the highest degree: women who looked like Mah-Jong, men who were the spitting images of the most handsome Cupanes and the most striking Ziinos, the incredible *grascia* of the long green overcoats, the sweat running down behind the pomaded ringlets; the goatish stink, the shrill oriental cries when the train moved, the women who fell to the ground beating the air with their feet, the extraordinarily intense vitality emanating from those gleaming eyes – all this made many things clear to the Monster, even including the periodical massacres carried out, in Kovno itself, by the Russians in all their wisdom.*

This is but one of the episodes observed by the ever-vigilant Monster during the last few days. The many others, including his stirring adventures along the various frontiers – Polish, Estonian and Soviet – will be the subject of extensive dramatic narration during the long winter evenings, to the accompaniment of your Fartfunken.*

The Monster is going out: he is going to view Botticelli's illustrations of the *Divine Comedy*, and also to chew the rag in the various *Radiogeschäfte*.*

And Lucio? I know he is having some sort of affair with Ferro. Regards to Aunt and to Giovanna. Tell Kiki that I have decided to eat her in the winter with an excellent Russian sauce made from herrings and tomato. Good wishes. The adventurous Monster.

Regards to Gutierrez, to Sciara and to Mormino and Clara. Also for Ing. Pagano. And to O.S. if he is still with us.

Regards to Pintacuda.*

The Monster has eaten excellent spaghetti with ham in a Lithuanian restaurant car between Riga and the Soviet frontier. Spaghetti is now international: *Laus nobis!**

Reply to the Hôtel Roter-Hahn.

Munich.*

NOTES
On paper headed "Koburger Hotel-Berlin N.W.". Two numbered sheets, four sides.

p. 145, *HF light*: "HF" stands for "high frequency".

p. 145, *Mormino*: The name of an engineer in Palermo.

p. 145, *calembours*: "Puns" (French).

p. 146, *the Baltic baroness... her famous mother*: Alessandra ("Licy") Wolff Stomersee and her mother Alice Barbi respectively.

p. 146, *a very abundant harvest there*: Lampedusa may have slipped in a "*calembour*" here, as the Italian word used for "harvest" is "*messe*" which in German means "exhibition" or "trade fair".

p. 146, *kulebyaka... obscene jokes on the name*: Kulebyaka is a pasty containing fish, meat or cabbage, with a covering of puff pastry. The first part of the word is very similar to the Italian word "*culi*", which means "backsides".

p. 146, *Vathek*: A reference to William Beckford's Gothic novel *Vathek* (1782).

p. 147, *Kovno*: The old name of the Lithuanian city of Kaunas, where the Warsaw-Riga train halted.

p. 147, *Mah-Jong... Cupanes... Ziinos... grascia... in all their wisdom*: For Mah-Jong, see note to p. 15. The Cupanes were a family of landowners in the district of Capo d'Orlando, members of the Bellini Club. The Ziinos were an eminent middle-class Palermitan family. Both the families were distinguished by their hooked noses. "*Grascia*" means "greasiness" or "muckiness" in Sicilian dialect. The "periodical massacres" carried out by the Russian is an allusion to the pogroms.

p. 147, *Fartfunken*: A "fart-emitter", word play on "Telefunken", Casimiro's radio.

p. 147, *Radiogeschäfte*: "Radio stores" (German).

p. 148, *Lucio... Pintacuda*: "Lucio" is a reference to Lucio Piccolo. "Ferro" is Pietro Ferro, a composer and the future director of the Conservatorio di Palermo. Lucio Piccolo had studied music under his predecessor, Antonio Savasta. For "Aunt and Giovanna" see third note to p. 8. "Kiki" is probably one of the dogs belonging to the Piccolos. "Gutierrez" is a reference to Gutierrez Spadafora, Prince of Spadafora, member of the Bellini Club (see also third note to p. 5). "Sciara" is Francesco Notarbartolo di Sciara, member of the Bellini Club and one of Lampedusa's best friends before his mental illness became apparent. For "Mormino" see second note to p. 145. Clara was his wife. The reference to Ingegner Pagano could not be identified. For "O.S." see note to p. 15. "Pintacuda" is Michele Pintacuda, landowner, musician and man of letters.

p. 148, *The Monster has eaten... Laus nobis*: The greetings to Pintacuda and the culinary notes are added, inside a double-bordered box drawn with pen and ink, in the top-right corner of the second-sheet recto. "*Laus nobis*" means "thanks to us" (Latin).

p. 148: *Hôtel Roter-Hahn... Munich*: The new address is written across the back of the second sheet.

XXIX

Date uncertain – Written at various stages

In times past the Monster would have spoken in his letters of the Dürers in Nuremberg or of the admirable Watteaus in the Alte Galerie, or again of the Manets, Cézannes and Renoirs, Menzels and von Maréeses exhibited in this Neue Galerie with an almost maniacal prodigality. He would also perhaps have mentioned the charming little aquiline noses of the Nurembergers and the truly metropolitan legs of the *Berliner Kinder.**

Alas, no longer! Radio has taken the place of painting and lovers with you; you appreciate no lines but the supple ones of the valves (shielded, of course), and you are said to abandon yourself to the unchaste embraces of those magnanimous copper tubes which gleam in the depths of the radio set.

And so, Radio. My goodwill will have to make up for my lack of knowledge. Shops selling this lovable invention are about as abundant in Germany as tobacconists with us. More in the provinces, however, than here in Berlin. Besides, every *grand magasin* has its vast *Radio Abteilung**. Some of these shops are put together with indescribable taste and luxury: there is one here entirely of matt gold with hidden orange lights which is a real delight... for the eyes. It is obvious

151

that Signor Di Leo* had no say in fitting it out. No counters at all, but internally illuminated crystal cubes support the squat menacing beasts. Temples, real temples full of a divine atmosphere and silence. Yes, silence. Because, with admirable shrewdness, the sets are tried out in separate soundproof rooms, where the croaking in one is not disturbed by the *piriti** in the other. Also, a wise municipal ordinance forbids loudspeakers in the public streets.

Now the sets. First of all, during the week I have been here I have not managed to see one which was not German. National products dominate the market, with Telefunken in the lead. Then there are certainly infinitely fewer large and powerful sets than with us. Sets between 100 and 200 marks reign supreme. I think that here Radio has by now gone beyond that stage which we might call "aristocratic", at which it still is with us, and has more or less penetrated into the population at large. In short, like motor cars here and in England. That may also be the result of the closely knit network of good stations.

It's also worth observing that Radio has in no way replaced orchestras in the cafés. Here every café, restaurant or confectioner's has its orchestra, always good, often numerous; quite a few premises on several floors have two or three. I have never heard a radio in a café! Nor can it be said that this is for reasons of profit, because here the Italian "supplement for the orchestra" does not exist. On the other hand I have been in one café (Trumpf) from which they were transmitting, and I can give you a brief account so that you may relive the scene, as you hear, with your eyes too.

A hall as large as the canopy of Palermo's Central Station – divided however by convenient stairways, landings and recesses in such a way as to eliminate this idea of overwhelming grandeur. It is covered in green marble streaked with red up to the waist, and above that in encaustic tiling of a lighter green with golden spangles. Ceiling of smooth gold. All around there is a wooden colonnade, also green. Nebuchadnezzar's dining room. In the middle, an open space for couples to dance in. A wall entirely of glass reveals Kurfürstendamm, its myriad lights, its crazy traffic, the incredible rain. In one corner, microphones at their noses, the orchestra: 15 men and women wearing – in contrast with the solemnity of the hall – peach-coloured shirts, soft collars, black ties and *champagne* trousers (or skirts). They play admirably – in a rounded, warm and melting tonality – the 'Blue Danube' at least twice an evening. After every piece, ecstatic applause. Sometimes the cellist (yes, he), without getting up, sings short pieces of song in a baritone voice. The current craze is *'Ich bin ganz für Liebe aufgemacht'*.* The audience *"jauchzt, jubelt, klappert, wird tollwütig"*.* He does not even thank them: he sings the song again.

(You should know that it is very fashionable to interrupt the music so that the violins may do imitations of birdsong, which you, down there in the Island of Fire, would take for nightingales.) All that goes on until 3, but the Monster cuts it short much earlier, spends about half an hour on the bus and goes back to the hotel.

Everything is large in this café: the faces of the regulars are as big as *bagghi*,* the backsides of their companions are mountains; they take out suitcase-sized cigar cases and extract cigars (*würzige Stumpen*)* which look like umbrellas; the *Schoppen** of beer is an ocean, and the slices of chocolate cake are lighthouses beaten by waves of cream. The amount these people eat is horrifying: one would think

153

they never did anything else; and one can appreciate, seeing them at the trough, the heroism with which they lasted out through four years of blockade and hunger.

But their indecency is also great. I am not speaking of the innumerable trollops who here, as the world over (with the *unique* exception of Palermo), hang about on the pavements and in the cafés, but of the overly elegant and overly shaven lads who sit and sigh at the corner tables until an old fat man, flushed and pop-eyed, decides to write something (what, ye Gods?) on the back of the bill and send a waiter with it to one of them. After that they sit at the same table and ten minutes later they go out together. And this in any respectable and commonplace café, frequented by very dignified old ladies and entire families including little boys, little girls and maidservants.

And the nude magazines on sale at every corner! And they are not artistic, because the real shops and the serious bookstalls do not stock them, and also because (as far as I know) there is no art to justify a whole issue of *Körper* dedicated to the *Menschliches Organ*!* Don't you agree?

Well – it is a large country, and the zeal with which they pursue every activity to the extreme, and the desire for the absolute which always animates them, are worthy of real consideration.

Then there are the shadowy parks, the beautiful, austere streets in Friedrichstadt, the elegance of Sans-Souci, the four-storeyed bookshops, the Landwehrkanal, in which a dismembered corpse is found every week, 112 aeroplane flights a day, an incredible ferment of life: within ten years they will, I think, send every nation a note, by means of the waiter…

* * *

Need I say that the Monster is in his element here? No one feels as much as he does the *Großstadt Pathos:** in the evening – when he goes back on the railway, which is partly elevated as in New York, and sees below him kilometres of empty streets, flooded with rain, with an endless line of lamps and every now and then a shunting station with a tangle of rails and green, red and white lights – he feels such bitter, *poignantes** and delightful emotions as a hundred of Böcklin's sunsets* could not give him. This is the true romanticism of today!

And the workmen in their leather jackets shining with the rain, and the continual rumble of the trains, and the sublime metropolitan crowd in which every face, for those who take the trouble to look, is a poem of suffering and unease – a unique suffering and unease, remember, of a quality which history has not known before now.

I have to say that no city I know is more clearly, more cruelly, a metropolis. Paris's French gaiety and London's bonhomie being absent, we are left with the hard lines of a gigantic construction. Nothing is harder than this city, although at every step it looks at you with the laughing eyes of a young girl.

And the characters, the strange characters! The street sweepers with their professorial spectacles, the fat female hawkers with the newspapers pinned to their skirts, the *Schupo** as steadfast as statues under the downpour. And above all a kind of army of very weird individuals, scattered everywhere, who from their appearance seem to be caricatures of Giosuè Carducci,* and who are hanging about everywhere without doing or saying anything in particular! Who are they? Bolshevik spies, a rare subspecies of pederast, the preparation for a *réclame* about a head lotion?

The Monster is now leaving for the North. But this is still his address: his long labour calls for a reply. He hopes that the enclosed magazines and cards will serve to keep him in high esteem with Barba, di Leo and Mormino. To Mormino, including Clara* the Monster sends his regards –

The Berlin Monster

I was forgetting about the Jews, who would deserve a whole chapter. But I believe I shall see more appetizing ones in Livonia.*

NOTES

On paper headed "Koburger Hof-Berlin N.W.". Four numbered sheets, eight sides. The letter, from Berlin, can be dated September 1930.

p. 151, *Dürer... Berliner Kinder*: The painters mentioned in this paragraph are Albrecht Dürer, Antoine Watteau, Édouard Manet, Paul Cézanne, Pierre-Auguste Renoir, Adolf von Menzel and Hans von Marées. "*Berliner Kinder*" means "Berliners" (German).

p. 151, *every grand magasin has its vast Radio Abteilung*: Every "shopping centre" (French) has its vast "radio section" (German).

p. 152, *Signor di Leo*: Probably a radio-shop owner in Palermo.

p. 152, *piriti*: "Farts" (Sicilian).

p. 153, *Ich bin ganz für Liebe aufgemacht*: "I Am All Ready for Love" (German). The song has not been identified.

p. 153, *jauchzt, jubelt, klappert, wird tollwütig*: "Exults, rejoices, claps, goes wild" (German).

p. 153, *bagghi*: "Farms with courtyards" (Sicilian).

p. 153, *würzige Stumpen*: "Aromatic half-cigars" (German).

p. 153, *Schoppen*: "Half-pint glass" (German).

p. 154, *Menschliches Organ*: "Human organ" (German).

p. 155, *Großstadt Pathos*: "Metropolitan pathos" (German).

p. 155, *poignantes*: "Poignant" (French).

p. 155, *Böcklin's sunsets*: A reference to the symbolist Swiss painter Arnold Böcklin.

p. 155, *Schupo*: Abbreviation of *Schutzpolizei*, "City police" (German).

p. 155, *Giosuè Carducci*: Giosuè Carducci was a very influential poet and educator, and the first Italian to win the Nobel Prize for Literature in 1906.

p. 156, *Barba... Clara*: Barba was the owner of a radio and gramophone shop in Via Rosolino Pilo, in Palermo. For Di Leo see first note to p. 152, and for Mormino see second note to p. 145. Clara was Mormino's wife.

p. 156, *I was forgetting... Livonia*: Added in the bottom left corner of the fourth-sheet verso, circumscribed by a line drawn in ink.

Appendix

I

My adorable Pony. I received yours yesterday, dated the 23rd.

The description of the "Sardinian dwarf donkeys" moved me. I knew they would be all the rage. Have you ever heard ordinary English people complain about having eyes as beautiful as theirs! *Sweet little things*! As to having them in the *drawing room*, that is something which has virtually happened, because *ta mère** is there already. However, their future in England is assured, and they will certainly replace the ponies.

Here the celebrations for the Prince* have taken place in the following order. The first evening, a dinner and reception at the Town Hall. The square was well illuminated, that is the fountain,* which is all decorated along the borders.

It wasn't bad! A characteristic Spanish note. The nuns of Santa Caterina behind the gilt bars of the convent. The next evening they could be seen at Clementina's.* I was hoping for some decorations and renovations – they have not even added a lamp to the stairway – not even the Heir to the Throne could conjure away their centuries-old meanness! It seems that Clementina has not *séché** extravagant words and opinions. On the last day, lunch at Trabia's.* In the yellow ballroom – a table of honour – and four tables in the corners. It seems to have been indeed a marvel of taste and splendour.

The Prince was so bewitched by it that the King felt himself obliged to telegraph the Senator. I think the Prince must have thought with regret that – both men not being of the highest class – Yolanda might have been better off marrying Giuseppe.* Then that ancient Florian monument* gave a tea party at the Villa Igiea, and immediately afterwards a private dinner at Gangi's – there were only 20 people at the dinner, and as many afterwards. There was nothing much of anything. In the end Giulia Gangi* was screwed by Clementina, and an attempted *curtig** was blocked and smothered, at least for now.

On Wednesday there was the Scaletta-Bordonaro wedding* – after the death of Bissana's father, who is the bridegroom's first uncle. But that was not talked about – all being put off until the spouses were already on the open sea.

San Marco and Oddo have left by aeroplane for Rome, and have now been nicknamed "Amundsen" and "De Pinedo" respectively.* On 30th Papa will send you money with a breakdown.

Congratulations on your treatment's good results.

I have had a reply from Aix. The terms are good – full board for 60 francs, 66 with the extras – which would come to 46 Italian lire. At the International. Papa was the one who suggested it.

Warm greetings to Uncle and Aunt* – endless big kisses for you from the Swiss sanatorium where Beatrice is.*

Cocò's wife has had to *libertarisi* – a good American,* she will go by aeroplane.

Trabia, for the love of Aesthetics, was obliged to invite *everyone* – Fascists, Christians, radicals, liberals and masons.

Your invitation has been sent.

NOTES

Beatrice Lampedusa, mother of Giuseppe, is writing to her son who was in London. This eccentrically written letter does not belong to the Fondazione Biblioteca di via Senato, but is part of the correspondence held by Lampedusa's heirs. Two folded sheets of graph paper, six sides.

p. 161, *ta mère*: "Your mother" (French).

p. 161, *the Prince*: Umberto di Savoia.

p. 161, *the fountain*: The fountain in Piazza Pretoria, facing the monastery church of Santa Caterina's convent.

p. 161, *Clementina's*: Clementina Trigona, first cousin of the Piccolos and Lampedusa. Her mother, Giulia Mastrogiovanni Tasca Filangeri di Cutò, was a lady-in-waiting to Queen Elena, and as a child Clementina played in the gardens of the Quirinale. A photograph shows her with the Princesses Yolanda and Mafalda of Savoy and Prince Umberto in their early childhood.

p. 161, *séché*: "Been sparing of" (Franco-Sicilian term).

p. 161, *Trabia's*: See second note to p. 5. He is the "Senator" in the following paragraph.

p. 162, *Giuseppe*: Giuseppe Lanza di Trabia, firstborn of Pietro and Prince of Scordia. The allusion is to the marriage of Yolanda of Savoy with Count Bergolo – who, just like the Lanza di Trabia family, was not a great nobleman.

p. 162, *that ancient Florian monument*: Franca Florio, one of the most celebrated local beauties of the Belle Époque, for whom Beatrice had little tenderness. There was a rumour that Beatrice Lampedusa had had an affair with Franca Florio's husband, the financier Ignazio Florio. The "ancient Florian monument" is therefore a snide reference to Franca Florio's faded beauty.

p. 162, *Gangi's… Giulia Gangi*: Palazzo Gangi in Piazza Croce dei Vespri. It was in the rooms of this palace that Luchino Visconti set the ball in his film version of *The Leopard*. Giulia Gangi was the wife of Giuseppe Mantegna, Prince of Gangi, owner of the Palazzo Gangi.

p. 162, *curtig*: Short for *"curtigghiu"*, Sicilian term for social intrigues.

p. 162, *the Scaletta-Bordonaro wedding*: The wedding between Gabriele Bordonaro and Anna Papè della Scaletta.

p. 162, *Bissana's father*: Michele Spadafora, Duke of Bissana, father of Gutierrez. See first note to p. 148.

p. 162, *San Marco... respectively*: "San Marco" is a reference to Stefano Lanza Filangeri, Count of San Marco. "Oddo" is Ugo Oddo, friend of Fulco Santostefano della Verdura (see note to p. 46) and, like him, an exile in Paris. The Norwegian explorer Roald Amundsen had undertaken a flight to the North Pole in May 1925, and the aviator Francesco De Pinedo had carried out a transcontinental flight on the same year.

p. 162, *Uncle and Aunt*: Pietro and Alice Tomasi della Torretta.

p. 162, where Beatrice is: The phrases which follow run along the margins, around the written page, making a frame for it.

p. 162, *Cocò's wife has had to libertarisi – a good American*: A reference to Peggy Hirsch, wife of Corrado (Cocò) Valguarnera, Prince of Niscemi. Cocò was the elder brother of Raimondo Valguarnera, whom Tomasi calls Raimondo Arenella, because of the family title of Duke of Arenella. See also second note to p. 6. *"Libertarisi"* means "slip away" (Sicilian) and possibly, in this case "unburden herself" (of her pregnancy).

II

My dearest Aunt,
At the very moment I was about to send our greetings telegram, I was given your letter.

I think good old Riccobono* has exaggerated a little:
Mama does eat enough, goes out, keeps occupied and is
cheerful, but she is certainly no longer in the same rosy
health in which she was even three months ago. Mainly as
a result of an intermittent irritation of the mouth (aphtha),
which bothers her and irritates her very much.

She has tried several remedies with varying results, but
on no account is she willing to consult a doctor; besides, she
says she has no confidence in anyone but Coniglio.*

There is no doubt whatsoever that a few days in the
country, with good air and good company, would do her a
lot of good, and she has often mentioned this. And it would
also give us an opportunity to consult Coniglio.

But, I repeat, there is no question in any way of a
situation which is even remotely worrying, and she is well
aware of the distressing times you have gone through.

Anyway, if you can invite her, it will please her very much,
and she will certainly come. Grateful and keen though I am,
I could only manage a *weekend*.

But you must write directly to Mama because, of course, I cannot show her your letter or tell her that you have written to me; she would be frightened, and above all poor old Riccobono would be undeservedly despised!

Like everyone, we have had some very anxious days at the end of September – even more serious for me if you consider that Licy* found herself (and still finds herself) isolated in the depths of the countryside and unable to travel.

Fortunately she is now recovering, and we hope she will be able to undertake the return journey within a few days.

I shall write to Lucio shortly and thank him for the good lifelike photograph.

I am really glad to hear that your affairs are reaching a happy solution; poor Rosenstingl* has done everything he could, but the political situation was against him.

But he has not given up all hope of success.

In expectation of your good news and thanking you very much for your affectionate solicitude, I send most affectionate greetings to you and all the family

Giuseppe

NOTES

Two folded sheets of graph paper, six sides. The date is underlined. The letter, addressed to Aunt Teresa Piccolo (see third note to p. 8), is in the Fondazione Biblioteca di via Senato's collection.

p. 165, *Riccobono*: A well-to-do dealer in building materials. Often resorted to by the local aristocracy, also in his capacity as a moneylender.

p. 165, *Coniglio*: Trusted doctor of the Piccolos at Capo d'Orlando. On request he would also visit them in Palermo.

p. 166, *Licy*: Alessandra Wolff Stomersee, Giuseppe Tomasi di Lampedusa's wife. See fifth note to p. 141.

p. 166, *Rosenstingl*: A Jew who took refuge in Palermo in 1937, the year before Mussolini's Racial Laws. He was the librarian of Pietro Emanuele Sgadari di Lo Monaco (Bebbuzzo). See note to p. 15. Rosenstingl managed to emigrate to Spain and opened an antique shop in Barcelona.

III

Dear Erede,

Thank you for your letter which I have just received, with a stamp (who knows why?) from Sestri Levante. I hasten to tell you that on this occasion my mind has been working extremely well, whatever you try to hint: I passed through Genoa at 4 in the morning, and to me it would have seemed cruel and pointless to keep you awake until that hour.

I shall always be glad to hear any interesting items you have to tell me. If they are matters which concern me, or *almost* concern me, I beg you to tell me immediately.

I leave on Monday for London.

Best wishes to you and yours, and especially to you,

Giuseppe Tomasi

(London address:
D.o.P. c/o Marchese della Torretta
Italian Ambassador
20 Grosvenor Square, London

NOTE
Postcard. D.o.P. refers to Lampedusa's title of Duke of Palma.

169

IV

London, 29th May [1925]

20 Grosvenor Square

Dear Erede,

I have been here for three days. Superbly accommodated, exquisitely fed, constantly chauffeured, I really am living the life of Riley. You cannot imagine just how dizzying, terrifying and fascinating London is. A most delightful inferno. All the best, yours,

G. Tomasi

NOTE
Postcard. Lampedusa arrives in London for the first time on 26th May 1925, staying at the Italian Embassy in London. He is overawed by the metropolis. His "journey through Europe" starts here.

V

London, 19th June 1925

Dear Erede,

I have received your letter, which gave me great pleasure. I shall reply in detail soon. At the moment I am in Richmond, the latest territory "annexed" by London. (So now this monster of a city measures 42 km from north to south.)

As you can see, this is a veritable paradise. Weather splendid.

Affectionately
yours,

Giuseppe Tomasi

NOTE

Postcard. Lampedusa continues to be astonished at the sight of the metropolis. But if the city in May was a "most delightful inferno", it is now "a veritable paradise".

VI

Dear Erede,
I'm leaving tomorrow for Belgium. I still have not managed to find a single second to answer your letter properly.

   I will try.

                    Best wishes

                                        G. Tomasi

Giuseppe Tomasi – poste restante – Brussels

NOTE
The postcard shows Holborn's "Old Houses", also known as "Staple Inn, Holborn Bars", describing it as "one of the few symbolic landmarks of the past history of London".

VII

Dear Erede,
Here I am at last in Paris. So you may reply to me if you wish.

Paris is lovely. But it is in a state of latent Bolshevism. It looks like Italy in '19. This morning another Communist slipped into the banking district – while I was cashing a modest *chèque* – with cries of "Down with!" and threats and stones. And no one reacted. Oh! Mussolini!

* * *

I shall be in Italy in September, but only for a few days because I am going to leave for Austria with my mother.

* * *

After careful observations carried out in London, Brussels, Antwerp and here, I am in a position to announce that pederasty has made immense progress. If we go on at this rate, then in a hundred years a man who has physical relations with a woman will be a museum piece. To avoid any misunderstanding, I must give you to understand that the Mimì whom I mentioned in my letter from Brussels did turn

177

out, after careful and thorough investigation, to be without any doubt of the female sex.

* * *

The way the decorative arts find their expression here is very interesting. One could say that modern art is at last on the right road. In fact much of the architecture and furnishing is very beautiful. Yet even this, like the demonstrations and the pederasty, is the result of Bolshevism. That Italy is not Bolshevik in the slightest can be seen in its horrible pavilion in the classical style with an interminable Latin inscription. (To appreciate how horrible it is, just consider that the exhibition is deliberately based on an almost Futuristic programme.) Thank goodness we have Bottecchia and Ascari.

Affectionate regards,

G. Tomasi

NOTE

Letter sent from Paris. Written two days before Letter I, this one deals with some of the same themes: the "latent Bolshevism" of Paris and Mussolini's appeal. The ubiquitousness of homosexuality, which is also attributed to Bolshevism, is another theme developed by Lampedusa in some of the letters of this period. Lampedusa seems to be attracted by Futurism, which was the theme of the Italian Pavilion at the World Fair in Paris. "Bottecchia" is a reference to the cyclist Ottavio Bottecchia, who won the Tour de France in 1924 and 1925; "Ascari" is a reference to the motor-racing champion Antonio Ascari, who died on the Montlhéry track the day after this letter was written.

VIII

Optime Maxime,

Since I left Paris I have not slept two consecutive nights in the same bed, and so I could not send you my address. Meanwhile my article is almost finished; I should like to send it to you as soon as possible, but I do not know whether you are in Genoa or elsewhere. I am leaving tomorrow for Lyon and the Auvergne, but I shall come back here again. So please write to me here with your permanent address and I shall send you the article.

In the middle of September I am going back to Italy (Alto Adige). I have seen some magnificent things which I shall describe to you at length when I am less tired.

I am sleepy just now and it's in my mind that I must be on the train by 6 tomorrow.

So I look forward to your news and your address

G. Tomasi

NOTE

Postcard. *Optime Maxime* is a Latin pun: "My dear Massimo" and "Best and greatest (friend)".

IX

[September 1925?]

Dear Erede,
Where are you? My article is ready and all I need is your
precise address in order to send it to you. Sincerely,

G. Tomasi

NOTE
Postcard from Bolzano.

X

Dear Erede,
I am here in Florence. If you happen to be in Pisa, please let me know.

I shall be here until the end of the month.
Yours sincerely,

G. Tomasi

NOTE
Postcard.

XI

Bolzano, 15th September 1926

Dear Erede,

This morning I got your letter from Dijon and your postcard together. I have come down here through the Brenner Pass after a long journey.

I have sent the article today by recorded delivery and I hope it will reach you at the same time as this letter. I shall not write to you at length because my ink is white. I am planning a letter of monumental proportions. Rolandi-Ricci's photographs are already stuck in my album. I have sent them to be developed again and I'll send them to you.

All best wishes. Send me news of yourself and of the article. I shall be here a long time.

G. Tomasi

The "article" Lampedusa is referring to in this postcard is his essay 'W.B. Yeats and the Irish Renaissance', which was published in *Le Opere e i Giorni* (Year 5, No. 11, 1st November 1926) under the name Giuseppe Tomasi di Palma. Massimo Erede was the brother-in-law of Nella Capocaccia, daughter of Mario Capocaccia, the editor of the magazine's review section. The editor-in-chief was Mario Maria Martini. Many important authors, such as Eugenio Montale, Riccardo Bacchelli and Camillo Sbarbaro, had some of their writings published there.

XII

[18th September 1926]

Bolzano. Hôtel Stiegl.

Most illustrious Erede,
I do hope that my article has reached you by now. It was well and truly finished by the end of August. But, since I had already left when your postcard arrived at Dijon, and it then pursued me through various cities until it caught up with me here, there has been a delay of about two weeks.

If it happens to be published, I should like to know if more articles are needed and when. I am not saying this with a morbid mania for seeing my name in print again and again, but in order to know from the start when the work needs to be ready, so that I shall be *forced* to work – otherwise I wouldn't do anything.

And you, with your incomparable tact, will also be able to raise the question of payment. It's not that I believe my articles are worth much more than a packet of Macedonias, but because it would give me great satisfaction to earn even ten lire a year by my own efforts.

But if this is not standard practice, we shall say no more about it.

* * *

After leaving London at the start of August, I have wandered about extensively in France, seeing very beautiful things everywhere and relishing the latest cuisine and some girls who, although not ethereal and unattainable like those my dear Yeats talks about, were not for that reason any less agreeable.

But all these diversions have distressed my purse considerably; so that for the time being I am here, a place which is at the same time pleasant and cheap, and where I can concentrate on my personal financial deflation.

According to my calculations, the stabilizing of my lira should be complete towards the tenth of October, which is the date when I shall begin to be seaworthy once more.

My family are in Montecatini, but they will leave shortly for either Venice or here. If they come here, of course, my financial convalescence will be more rapid, and then I too may go to Venice and admire the last flickers of the famous "September" season.

The weather is freakishly fine and hot, and truly exceptional.

Of course nothing has been done with the London necktie; but when I am able to tell you or write to you about the extraordinary adventures which happened to me between Rolandi-Ricci's departure from London and mine, I am sure you will regard me as excused.

My regards to you and your family.

G. Tomasi.

NOTE
Letter from Bolzano.

XIII

Dear Erede,
This coming Saturday, 2nd October, I shall be in Venice. If
you want to give me some news of my article (or rather tell
me simply if you have received it, which I do not know), you
can write to me there, addressing the letter to:

Giuseppe Tomasi-Lampedusa
Hotel Manin, Venezia

My family are staying here for a few more days, and then
they are going to Bologna, where I shall join them towards
the 10th.
My very best wishes

G. Tomasi

NOTE
Postcard.

XIV

Bolzano, 1st October [1926]

Dear Distinguished Person,
Yesterday I had only just posted the card in which I asked you for some news of my article when your letter from Rocca Grimalda reached me.

I thank you heartily for your interesting news and for the truly friendly interest which you take in my affairs and for which I am very grateful.

Please thank M.M.M. for his kind words and for his even kinder intentions.

But my article? Will they publish it? And when?

Yesterday I informed you of my imminent departure for Venice: today I must deny that.

I was going to Venice partly to be some company for my aunt, who was there alone and was rather miffed, given that my uncle was delayed in London by matters of importance; and partly in order to visit Lajolo.

But since he has not bothered to reply to me even to let me know whether he was in Venice as I asked him, and since my aunt has telegraphed me that she was leaving for Salsomaggiore, I have cancelled that trip.

Instead next Sunday, 3rd October, I shall leave for Bologna together with my family.

In Bologna my address will be Hotel San Marco, Via Indipendenza.

* * *

I should very much like to go to Genoa for a few days. And I shall probably do that towards the 10th of this month.

You must tell me if you will be around on that date, or when you can be there.

I hope I shall be able to get something out of it (I am not speaking of financial considerations, which are after all secondary).

* * *

Given your interest in *Roma*, I can tell you that she had a narrow escape, given that on her maiden voyage she had on board one of the most accomplished Jonahs known.

My family thank you for your good wishes and reciprocate them, and my mother has asked to be remembered to your mother.

Please continue to send me your news (in Bologna) and accept once more my thanks and all good wishes.

G. Tomasi

NOTE

Letter from Bolzano. The transatlantic liner *Roma* started on her maiden voyage on 21st September 1926, on a route from Genoa to Naples and New York, and in December of that year, after picking up an SOS signal from a sailing ship which was sinking a hundred miles east of Madeira, she intervened to rescue the crew.

XV

6th [October 1926]

Dear Erede,

As you can see, I am still here. The weather is so fine that we have postponed our departure for a week. On Friday however I shall be in Bologna at the Hotel San Marco. And perhaps this coming Tuesday, 12th October, or thereabouts, I shall come to Genoa.

Please write to me in Bologna and let me know if you will be in town on that date. I shall telegraph the exact day of my arrival, and perhaps you would be so kind as to book me a room, at the Bavaria of course.

Nothing else to report.

Sincerely,

G. Tomasi

NOTE
Letter from Bolzano.

XVI

My dear Erede,

Many thanks for your best seasonal wishes. I did not answer your last letter mainly because it crossed with one of mine, but also because I was very embarrassed about what to reply to Capocaccia, as I had no article ready. I now hope to send one shortly.

Please ask Capocaccia himself whether M.M.M. has received one of my letters in which I sent him some verses by one of my cousins. I am asking this so that I can reply to the author who is nagging me daily. Thank you for the kind thought of collecting my writings in one volume: however, although there may be a publisher... there are no writings!

I am sorry you are not coming here after all: what can you do, it's too far. I hope there will be another time. I wish you for the New Year an income of 200,000 lire a month and 180 girls aged ten to sixteen at your disposal.

All the best,

G. Tomasi

NOTE
Letter from Palermo.

XVII

Dear Erede,

As you can see, I go on writing to you despite your disgraceful silence.

At the same time as you receive this letter you will receive my article, which I ask you to send to Capocaccia together with my regards. Please make him aware that this is the first part of an article which must, of necessity, be printed in two sections. In March I shall send the other part for possible publication on 10th April, since they want this present one for publishing on 1st March. (I think it is too late for February.)

The subject seems to me an interesting one, and perhaps it would be worthwhile to translate the whole book. Would you also please ask M.M.M. for some news of the poem I sent him; just so that I can reassure or finally discourage the soul in torment whom I have been incautious enough to arouse (*L'apprenti sorcier*). Best wishes. Perhaps we shall meet at Easter?

Yours,

G. Tomasi

NOTE
Letter from Palermo. *L'apprenti sorcier* (*The Sorcerer's Apprentice*) is the title of a famous poem by Goethe.

XVIII

My dear Erede,

I am sorry my last letter reached you at such a sad time. From what you have told me, your uncle was a forceful, intelligent man, and so now his loss will be the more grievous. Please convey to your father my sincere condolences.

I must thank you again for all the trouble which you are going to for me. I hope that I shall soon be able to send you the second part of my article, although it seems to me that there is still time enough.

Please thank Giovanninetti for his kind offer, which I am glad to accept: I should like to know, however (excuse my ignorance), if bimonthly means twice a month or once every two months, and also what should be the approximate length of the articles.

Let us hope that the negotiations over the translation are being concluded.

My friend is left in great perplexity by your reply concerning his verses, and also flattered because they have if nothing else been discussed; if you could give me some more particulars both he and I would be grateful.

* * *

My uncle's departure for London was a heavy blow. I don't know the reasons in any detail, because for some time he has been extremely reserved. But from the fact that he is the only one not to be retired but merely made available for transfer, and from other indications, I think that he will soon have an important post. But I am not the sort of person to let myself be thrown by one pied-à-terre less in London. And 24 hours after the news of the move I had already worked out a very detailed plan. I count on going to Spain; I would be leaving Genoa for Barcelona towards the middle of May, and indeed I would be grateful if you could let me know the cost of a first-class ticket, how many hours the crossing takes, and all the days on which the steamers sail.

I am sorry that you found Lajolo in a bad state. But in what sense? This is just one of the many enigmas in your letter.

We have had a shocking winter, with rain, winds and cold.

Please thank M.M.M., Capocaccia, and Giovanninetti on my behalf, and remember me to them. Best wishes to your family and a hearty handshake to you.

Yours,

G.T.

NOTE
Letter from Palermo.

XIX

5th March [1927]

Dear Erede,

I have your letter. I am still in bed, but I am getting up tomorrow: I have had a touch of influenza, not a bad one but protracted. If I add to this that from 10th to 20th February I have been in Tripoli, you will understand why my article is not yet ready. In any event by *the fifteenth* it will be in your hands. I hope that will be time enough. As soon as you receive the February issues, please send them to me.

Let me remind you that from 1st March there are great reductions in the railway fares to get here: I hope you will take advantage of that at Easter or thereabouts.

I shall write more to you when I can: for now I must devote myself completely to the article.

If not, there will be ructions.

All best wishes,

Giuseppe

PS: I have now received one issue of the magazine. I have found my article. However, there is a short section missing at the end: I hope they won't forget to publish it at the beginning of the second part: if they do forget, the thread will be lost.

NOTE
Letter from Palermo. Lampedusa had probably visited the first Trade Sample Fair in Tripoli (February–March 1927), organized by the Fascist government.

XX

Dear Erede,

I hope to get everything to you within a few days. Meanwhile, in the absence of the work I am sending you a picture of the workshop.

I hope to be in Genoa (for 24 hours) towards the middle of April.

Do not forget to tell me your news. My regards to your family.

Best wishes to you,

G. Tomasi

NOTE
A postcard showing the library of the Palazzo Lampedusa in Via Butera.

XXI

4th May [1927]

Dear Erede,

I have today received the issues of *Le Opere e i Giorni* containing my prose pieces. Believe me, it is a great satisfaction to see them printed; and I owe this satisfaction in large part to you and your kindness. If these two issues have been given free of charge by the magazine, please send me three more. If not, just one. Tell me if I ought to thank Capocaccia and Martini personally; or both of them.

And give me some indication if the 'Yeats' is welcome. All the best.

G. Tomasi

NOTE
Letter from Palermo.

Giuseppe Tomasi di Lampedusa in the gardens of
Villa Piccolo in the Autumn of 1956.

Giulio Fabrizio Tomasi,
Lampedusa's great-grandfather.

Beatrice Mastrogiovanni Tasca
di Cutò, Lampedusa's mother.

Beatrice, Teresa and Lina
Mastrogiovanni Tasca di Cutò.

Giulia Mastrogiovanni Tasca di Cutò,
Lampedusa's aunt.

Villa Lampedusa ai Colli, Palermo.

Palazzo Filangeri di Cutò, Bagheria.

Giuseppe Tomasi in the gardens of
Palazzo Filangeri di Cutò in 1903.

Giuseppe Tomasi in the gardens of
Palazzo Filangeri with the governess
Jeanne Sempell and Totò Ferraro.

Lampedusa at the time of his only
law exam in Rome in 1915.

Lampedusa at the time he enrolled for
a military training course to become
an auxiliary officer.

Casimiro and Lucio Piccolo (left and right respectively), Lampedusa's cousins, and the recipients of most of the letters in this volume.

Villa Piccolo at Capo d'Orlando in the 1930s.

Pietro Tomasi della Torretta,
Lampedusa's uncle.

Alice Barbi, Pietro Tomasi's
second wife and mother of
Lampedusa's future wife.

Stomersee Castle before
the 1905 fire.

Alice Barbi with her daughters
Alessandra (Licy) and Olga
(Lolette) at Stomersee.

Lampedusa during a trip to Riga
at the beginning of the 1930s.

Alessandra (Licy) Wolff,
Lampedusa's wife.

Licy and Giuseppe in Palermo
in the mid-1930s.

Lampedusa with Gioacchino Lanza
at the Castle of Montechiaro in
September 1955.

A letter from Lampedusa to Gioacchino Lanza Tomasi
dated 12th July 1957.

XXII

Dear Erede,

What's happened? Why this sudden silence?

Are you still planning to come here for Easter? (Next year.)

I shall be leaving in two weeks.

All best wishes,

G. Tomasi

NOTE

Postcard.

XXIII

Dear Erede,

I was delighted to get your letter with its interesting announcements. I see that soon we shall have to expel you from the most ancient and glorious order of celibates. Villain! Getting married to avoid paying the tax!*

I am very envious of your trip on Grappa; I only know this famous mountain by sight, having marvelled at it while it smoked, flashed and thundered from the other side of Val Brenta from early November to early December '17; in those days, however, I think that the most interesting display of fireworks was provided by us, from the Melette Mountains.*

You must also have enjoyed that adorable Vicenza, whose light, whose air, the beauty of whose houses and the filth of whose hotels are absolutely incomparable; it is by far the most mellow city in Italy; to live there and die there must be a delight without equal.

(This is just a rhetorical gesture: I should prefer to live in London and die nowhere.)

209

* * *

Mantua is certainly too melancholy. And there are too many mosquitoes. But no doubt you will have visited Isabella's Palace,* no longer squalid as in the first pages of *Perhaps Yes, Perhaps No*,* and you must have stayed in that round hall with its dome and its nocturnal frescoes by Giulio Romano,* where it must be so pleasant to lie in bed with a bedworthy woman, comparing her naked beauty to that of the naked goddesses on the ceiling.

I am glad you have decided on a profitable change of occupation. What southern shipyards are these? Naples, Castellammare or Palermo? I don't think there are any others. If everything turns out as I hope, I shall be in Genoa this coming Saturday, 4th June. I shall stay there until the morning of the next day and perhaps also the following Sunday just so as not to break the old habit of spending the festive days in Genoa (the ninth is the Unification).

Then I am leaving to go directly to London.

To our meeting again soon. I shall be more definite.

Regards and best wishes to your family,

G. Tomasi

Lajolo writes to me that he is in Genoa and that he will be there until 15th June.

NOTE

Letter from Palermo.

p. 209, *the tax*: A reference to the tax on celibacy, introduced by the Fascist government on 13th February 1927 in order to promote marriage and increase Italy's birth rate.

p. 209, *the Melette Mountains*: A group of mountains near Mount Asiago in the Veneto region, where Lampedusa and Erede were stationed during the First World War.

p. 210, *Isabella's Palace*: The Ducal Palace of Mantua.

p. 210, *Perhaps Yes, Perhaps No*: The last novel (1910) published by Gabriele D'Annunzio.

p. 210, *Giulio Romano*: The Italian painter and architect Giulio Romano.

XXIV

My dear Erede,

I am sending you my heartiest congratulations and most sincere good wishes for the happy event announced in your letter to me, which I received yesterday evening. Congratulations and good wishes which, I presume to say, are all the more precious since they come from the most earnest and diehard of all old bachelors. Besides, I am also convinced that there are people who cannot be happy except in marriage, and these people undoubtedly make up the most sensible and wholesome part of humanity.

For my part I am too much of a wanderer and of too fickle a temperament to compel any unhappy creature to go along with my fantasies.

This is at least the official reason for my persistent celibacy.

From today I am starting to lay aside the traditional *ventino* for the present. Since there are no *ventini* here, I shall put aside two lavish *pence*, to your distinct advantage.

When is the wedding? Not in winter I hope, because in those months it will be difficult for me to travel all through Italy to be there, as I would dearly have liked to do.

It's a rotten thing to accuse me of idleness. I am very weary with the excessive journeys I have undertaken these last few months; I have gone more than 1,500 km by rail and car, and by steamship on various lakes, I have visited 17 cities, and have also given a lecture in English on the connection between Italian poetry of the sixteenth century and that of Shakespeare and his followers. With great success, I may say, although I don't know whether this was due to the fascination of my eloquence or the fact that they did not understand a single word I was saying. And I have still not finished: the day after tomorrow I am leaving again to spend five days in a castle in Wales, invited *to hunt*! Now you know that in the matter of firearms I possess (or rather used to possess) only a certain familiarity with the 149-calibre howitzer, a very nice gun but not I think one generally used by huntsmen. You can imagine all the various possibilities of slaughter that are open to me. Besides, it doesn't matter: the castle enjoys the reputation of being one of the most beautiful around; it is chock-full of ghosts, like any respectable castle. You should know that, as a mark of honour, these English lords are accustomed to accommodate new guests precisely in their most haunted rooms. And let it be so: however, I hope the good Lord Powis will not be surprised if I keep all the lights on all night.

I shall soon be in Italy, towards 15th August; probably in Alto Adige.

Here, as always, it is raining.

Lajolo is in Genoa; or at least he was until twenty days ago, when I received a postcard from him in Edinburgh.

Dear Erede, I repeat my best wishes for the happiness of you and your bride, and I send you a hearty handshake.

G. Tomasi

NOTE

Letter from London. Lampedusa's invitation to Powis Castle appears here under a different light. He had cautiously avoided any mention of ghosts in Letter VIII, when writing to his spiritualist cousins. In Lampedusa's correspondence, as well as in the rest of his writings, truth is never the highest priority. The future novelist shows a much stronger inclination towards anecdotal fiction. *Ventini* were nickel coins.

XXV

Dear Erede,

What's happened to you? And why do you not come here by aeroplane, by steamer, by train or on foot?

Is it time now to send my best wishes for your wedding, or is it still too soon?

Sincerely yours,

G. Tomasi

NOTE

Letter from Palermo.

XXVI

Dear Giuseppe,
I am very touched by the interest you've shown in these cards – I must point out however that historical painting is the worst kind. This painting for example is frankly horrid, but it shows colours and costumes which haven't changed. You can even see the same chasubles as those in Assisi's collection from the time of St Francis here in the cathedral today. The lighting in a Russian church is always provided solely by candles and lamps, more or less as in St Mark's and during the time of the catacombs.

She is quite a good child, but with as little imagination as possible. – This portrays a miracle performed by St Nicholas at the time of the Tartars. Did you know that the Patron of Russia was an Italian?

André sends you his wishes and thanks you for your card, and we are all waiting to hear from you.

My respects to the Princess.

Let us know of your plans.

Best wishes,

L.

NOTE

Postcards from Licy, no date. These two postcards appear to have been sent together in one envelope and probably date back to before Lampedusa's first trip to Stomersee (1929–30). Licy's tone is still rather formal, and she is writing in French. The reference to the child has not been identified. The key to the picture on the first postcard indicates that the subject is the Patriarch Nikon, and the painter is Sergei Miloradovich. The key to the second says that the painter is Ilya Yefimovich Repin and the subject is St Nicholas Thaumaturgus.

Biographical Note

Giuseppe Tomasi di Lampedusa was born on 23rd December 1896 in Palermo, Sicily. At the turn of the century, the city was very much caught between the old and the new. On the one hand the wealthy entrepreneurs centring around the Florio family, on the other a handful of ancient, noble families, once at the height of their powers, then mostly in decline. The Lampedusas were one such family: they lived in a mansion which they maintained by occasionally opening it up to the public.

The Corberas of Salina in *The Leopard* are imbued with barely disguised autobiographical elements from Lampedusa's own idealized family history. Giulio Fabrizio Tomasi, the author's great-grandfather, was an amateur astronomer, a quiet man, notwithstanding his fits of temper, a little bigoted, with a few peculiar idiosyncrasies such as an inclination for science, but really altogether unexceptional. His son, Giuseppe Tomasi, the author's grandfather, wrote in his *Journal* that his father's villa mostly saw the comings and goings of the clergy, and hardly any social life. The family as he depicted it seems without any real ambition, and is a far cry from the fictional description of their descendant: there is nothing of the awesome patriarch in Giulio, who keeps himself at a distance from worldly pleasures and the world at large. His scientific gifts are also exaggerated in the novel – he had made no discoveries and was unrecognized in the scientific world, though his scientific library, mostly in French, was up to date.

The Lampedusas' reputation had been established by a single member of the Tomasi family – Prince Ferdinando Maria, who was mayor of Palermo in the mid-eighteenth century, and who brought the family to the fore of social and political life. Lampedusa's parents – Giulio Tomasi, duke of Palma, and his wife Beatrice Tasca di Cutò – had themselves great expectations, and Beatrice's dowry was large enough to warrant their ambitions. Beatrice was very much an unconventional product of Palermitan aristocracy. Her liberal education and wide reading set her apart: her influence on her son would be huge, and later cause no end of conflict with his wife, as the two women clashed over their claim on him. Beatrice encouraged and directed Lampedusa's cultural interests; they also travelled extensively together. His father, on the other hand, seemed to him cold and distant: Lampedusa felt rejected, and this marked him greatly.

Lampedusa's great-grandfather on his mother's side, Alessandro Filangeri di Cutò, married a Milanese singer, Teresa Merli Clerici, after the death of his first wife, and had only one legitimate heir, his daughter Giovanna, the author's grandmother. When Alessandro died in 1854, Giovanna was only four years old. Her tutor deemed it best to remove her and her mother from the unpleasant situation in Sicily, as her father's legacy was fought over, so Giovanna grew up and was educated in Paris. She only returned to Sicily in 1867, in order to marry Lucio Tasca di Almerita, the heir to a recent fortune. She had five daughters: Beatrice (Lampedusa's mother), Teresa (m. Piccolo), Nicoletta (also known as Lina, m. Cianciafara), Giulia (m. Trigona di

Sant'Elia) and Maria, who never married and eventually committed suicide. The five Cutò sisters – beautiful, rich, uninhibited and more educated than the average – also carried on part of their mother's eccentricity.

Giuseppe's aunt Lina died in the great Messina earth-quake of 28th December 1908. Only three years later, her sister Giulia was murdered by her lover, Vincenzo Paternò del Pugno, who then tried to shoot himself, but survived and was tried in Rome in 1912. This trial greatly affected the family, not least because the defence made a point of the shamelessness of the Cutò sisters, with their liberal education and idiosyncratic upbringing. Maria suffered greatly – so did Beatrice. As a result, Lampedusa's parents retired from the public eye, and the family home was closed to visitors and strangers.

Lampedusa was then sixteen. He completed secondary school at the Liceo Garibaldi in Palermo, getting his diploma in 1914. The following year, he enrolled at the University of Rome to study Law. His parents probably hoped he would follow in the footsteps of his uncle Pietro, a diplomat and in those days Italian plenipotentiary to the King of Bavaria – but Lampedusa never sat a single exam, either at the time or after the war, when he re-enrolled at the University of Genoa. In November 1915, he was called to arms, and signed up for an exclusive fast-track military training which allowed young men from good families to become auxiliary officers. He trained in Messina, and was appointed Corporal in May and assigned to a battery stationed in Augusta, under the command of Lieutenant Enrico Cardile, a man of letters with whom he became good friends. In 1917, Lampedusa trained at the Military Academy in Turin to become an officer, and was sent to the front in September, just a month before the famous Battle of Caporetto (24th October–19th November 1917), which was one of the greatest military defeats in Italian history. The Italian army suffered huge losses as they were pushed into retreat under the assault of the Austro-Hungarian forces. Lampedusa had been assigned to an artillery observation point on the slopes of Mount Asiago. As the enemy advanced, his station was cut off, and he was captured and taken prisoner by a company of Bosnian soldiers.

Not much is known about his time as a prisoner – Lampedusa was never very talkative about his private life, and said very little about this particular period. There are however a few memorable anecdotes, such as the time he allegedly went on a night-time tour of Vienna, which included a visit to the Opera, dressed up as an Austrian officer, having agreed with the real Austrian officer accompanying him that he would not attempt to escape, but refusing to give his word on it; or the time he did escape from Szómbathely, a prison camp in Hungary, again dressed as an Austrian officer, only to be apprehended at the Swiss border and threatened with the death penalty for desertion, until somebody realized he was an Italian prisoner of war in disguise.

Eventually, with the collapse of the Austro-Hungarian Empire, Lampedusa did manage to escape, and returned to Italy on foot about a year after he was taken prisoner. In 1919, he was once more serving his country in Casale Monferrato in the Piedmont region as a public-security officer dealing with the disturbances of the post-war period. He was finally dismissed in February 1920, after becoming a Lieutenant.

Little is known about his childhood friends or the aftermath of war, but there is no doubt that Lampedusa's love of literature was firmly established during this period. Alongside his friends Fulco Santostefano della Verdura and Lucio Piccolo, who was also his cousin, he read widely and avidly. Fulco introduced him to the great French poets – from Mallarmé to Verlaine and Valéry. Lampedusa had learnt French from his mother, and always maintained that he was fluent in German, which had been an essential part of his and his cousins' early education. However, although he admired German literature, he would never be passionate about it. His alleged fluency was really wishful thinking on his part: his German was poor, and no Austrian would have believed it was his mother tongue. The Viennese tour in disguise was probably just a figment of his imagination. Shortly after the end of the war and his imprisonment, he immersed himself in English literature. There are several copies of English classics in the Lampedusa library which date from between 1919 and 1922 and are signed "Giuseppe Tomasi di Palma". These must have been years of intense reading – years during which he became acquainted with Shakespeare, Coleridge, Trollope and Joyce among others, and the time when Lucio Piccolo dubbed him "the Monster", on account of his voracious reading habits.

At around the same time, Lampedusa suffered a serious nervous breakdown, and there were rumours that he was sexually impotent. He tried to get away from Palermo as much as possible: he regularly travelled around Italy with his mother, and often stayed with three comrades from his prison-camp days, who remained among his best friends. One of them, Massimo Erede, introduced him to Mario Maria Martini, the editor of a distinguished literary magazine.

Lampedusa's diplomat uncle, Pietro Tomasi della Torretta, had in the meantime left Bavaria to return to

Russia in 1917. He had been there previously at the start of his career. During his time in St Petersburg between 1899 and 1903, he had met Baroness Alice Wolff, née Barbi. She was the daughter of an Italian musician who had made a name for himself in Germany, and she herself had studied the violin, and then begun a highly successful concert career as a mezzo-soprano, becoming one of Brahms's favourite Lieder singers and presumably his mistress. In 1893, however, at the age of thirty-five, Alice Barbi abandoned her singing career and married Boris Wolff, a Baltic baron, with whom she had two daughters – Alessandra, born in 1894, and Olga, born in 1896.

Boris Wolff died in 1917, and in 1920 Pietro Tomasi married Alice, who was fifteen years his senior, and thus sardonically referred to as "the young Alice" by her sister-in-law Beatrice. In 1922, after having been Minister of Foreign Affairs and Senator of the Kingdom, Tomasi della Torretta was appointed Italian Ambassador in London, where he stayed until 1927, when he was removed because of his disagreements with the Fascist regime. In 1925, his nephew Giuseppe went to visit him. This would be the first of many trips to Britain.

During his several long-term stays in Britain, Lampedusa set out to reconcile the landscapes of his literary imagination with reality. His spoken English was awkward at best and, for all his reading, he had little actual experience of the world, preferring a novelistic take on life. Lampedusa travelled all over Britain – allegedly even getting engaged in Scotland. He would wander the streets of London searching for the city Dickens described, visit the places evoked by an author in order to relive his works, and even assert that a few verses from Burns were a foolproof method of courting girls. It should be noted that Lampedusa's Britain was very much that of his own social class: he had no contacts with the working classes, nor was he interested in the most parochial aspects of British life. Nevertheless, England would remain Lampedusa's ideal country.

Lampedusa travelled to Britain in 1925, 1926 and 1927, and again in 1928 and 1931, though by then he could no longer count on his uncle's hospitality, and his own fortunes had taken a turn for the worse. During his first trip to London in 1925, he had met Alessandra Wolff, also known as "Licy", the eldest daughter of his uncle's wife. She later said, of their first meeting, that having been left to their own devices by her parents, they headed towards Whitechapel talking about Shakespeare. Certainly their shared love of literature was an important factor in their relationship: both of them seemed to be people who had turned to literature as an escape from their inadequacy for real life.

Licy, however, was married, though at the time of that first meeting she was already separated from her husband, the Baron André Pilar, whom she had wed in 1918. One of the few tsarist officers to have survived the Battles of the Masurian Lakes, he spent most of his time between Riga and Germany in the Twenties. His marriage with Licy had been unhappy. Pilar was rumoured to be homosexual, and the early days of their union were tempestuous. As a result, Licy suffered a nervous breakdown, which was treated with insulin and, later, with psychoanalysis by Julius Felix Boehm, a pupil of Karl Abraham, the founder of the Psychoanalytical Society in Berlin, of Baltic origin (later Boehm was the head of the Goering Institute, the Psychoanalytical Association connected to the Nazis, and became a specialist in the treatment of homosexuals, many of whom he sentenced to death). This was Licy's first experience of psychoanalysis, which was to become her life's profession.

In later years, Licy claimed that it had been love at first sight between her and Lampedusa. Their surviving correspondence, however, suggests otherwise. Licy also claimed that Lampedusa visited her at Stomersee, the Wolffs' estate near the Latvian border with Estonia and Russia, two years after their first meeting in London. In fact, he appears to have made his first visit only in August 1930. That same year, the couple also met in Rome, where she was visiting her mother at his uncle's house in Via Brenta. Their romance developed quickly. Madly in love, Lampedusa sent her daily love letters full of Proustian reminiscences. In January 1932, while she was staying with her mother in Rome, Licy was invited to spend Easter in Palermo. They had decided to get married, and though their families had not been informed, they were certainly suspicious. In the meantime, Licy had obtained a divorce from Pilar, and Lampedusa had gathered all the necessary paperwork. They married in Riga on 24th August 1932.

On that same day, Lampedusa wrote to his parents announcing his decision. Naturally reserved and keen to avoid confrontation, he hoped to receive a congratulatory telegram, but five days later, having obtained no response, he sent an agonized letter to his mother. Licy, on the other hand, proved to be rather more independent from parental influence. Her family, who were also informed of the marriage as a *fait accompli*, immediately sent her their congratulations. Her mother's many questions, on the other hand, remained unanswered.

Eventually, both families met the couple in Bolzano in October. During this meeting, the signs of all future tensions were already evident. Beatrice had no intention of parting from her son, and opposed their plans to live in a separate apartment, while Licy insisted on their independence. Predictably, settling in Palermo proved difficult, and Licy soon returned to her Baltic estate. Lampedusa joined her in the summer and stayed well into the winter, then returned to Sicily for Christmas and tried to convince her to join him, but Licy refused with a harsh letter.

Things did not improve with the death of Lampedusa's father in 1934. In fact, the author was forced to stay even longer in Palermo to take care of the ongoing inheritance squabbles. The days of his European wanderings were over, and the couple remained apart, meeting a couple of times a year: eventually at Stomersee in the summer, in Rome for Christmas, and occasionally for shorter periods in Palermo. Licy's letters outnumber Lampedusa's. During those years she was often sick and presumably a hypochondriac. In 1936, Licy spent a long time in Italy, in order to become a member of the Italian Psychoanalytic Society. She was admitted without an exam, on the strength of a report on two clinical cases which had greatly impressed Edoardo Weiss, who had trained in Vienna in the Freudian circle and was then president of the society.

The couple's relationship was almost entirely epistolary. The long letters travelling back and forth from Latvia to Palermo generally avoided any topic that might cause friction: they included minute accounts of their diets, extensive commentaries and observations on their beloved dogs, travel notes and, on Lampedusa's part, detailed descriptions of encounters with mutual and approved acquaintances – though these were few and far between. Whenever the subject of resuming their life together in Palermo came up, Licy's replies were scathing, and she expressly stated that she would not bear her mother-in-law's interference.

The Second World War was devastating both for Lampedusa and for Licy, particularly because it brought the loss of their childhood homes, which had always been their refuge from the world outside. In December 1939, Lampedusa was recalled to arms. He went on a two-month refresher course and was mobilized before the war broke out, but managed to get himself discharged only three months later on account of rheumatoid arthritis in his right leg. In the meantime, after the Ribbentrop-Molotov Pact, Licy was forced to leave the Stomersee estate. She fought to save her belongings, and tried to obtain passports for some Jewish friends in Riga, but by the end of the year she had to flee to Rome. In 1941 she returned to Latvia, which had been occupied by German troops during the Siege of Leningrad. She visited Stomersee several times, sleeping in a tent. The castle had been ransacked, and the peasant population deported. She remained in Latvia until the end of 1942, when the Russian counter-offensive began.

Lampedusa displayed far less fighting spirit: he was resigned and despondent. He was once more entirely under the control of his mother, and spent most of his time with his cousins. Towards the end of 1942, both he and his mother moved in with the Piccolos at Capo d'Orlando. The Piccolos' residence was the only house where he would ever truly feel at ease after the family seat in Palermo was destroyed by the bombings. In November, Licy finally returned from Latvia, and Lampedusa joined her in Rome for Christmas, but went back to Sicily almost immediately. He was looking for a house near the Piccolos, not wanting to take further advantage of his cousins' hospitality. In 1943 he rented a house in Contrada Vina, and moved in with his mother. He frequently travelled to Palermo, constantly preoccupied with the fate of the family home in Via Lampedusa, which looked worse and worse for wear, but had yet to be directly hit.

In February, he once more tried to convince his wife to join him, but this was in vain. They continued their correspondence throughout 1943, their letters full of the horrors of the war. On 22nd March, a ship was blown up in Palermo's harbour. The debris that fell on the family home took the roof off the library room: many of the books in the Lampedusa collection still bear the traces, ingrained with soot and shrivelled with rainwater. On 5th April, the building was hit directly: Lampedusa surveyed the ruins and then headed to the villa of Stefano Lanza di Mirto in Santa Flavia on foot. He stayed there for three days, mute with shock and grief, before returning to Capo d'Orlando.

In July 1943, the rented house in Contrada Vina was also bombed while Lampedusa and his mother were out. By then, the Allied landings had started, and the coast was unsafe. Soon after, fearing a German invasion and the division of the country, Licy joined them in Capo d'Orlando, and the three moved inland to a house in Ficarra, a village in the surrounding hills, where they lived out the last days of the Allied invasion.

In mid-October, after the Armistice, the two families separated once more. It was the first time that the couple lived in Sicily on their own, without his mother. They moved to Palermo, while Beatrice remained in Ficarra. Shortly afterwards she moved into a hotel in Capo d'Orlando, where she would remain for two years. In 1946, she refused to go and live once more with her son, and moved back into a wing of the derelict family mansion on her own, where a few months later she died.

Between 1943 and 1946, Lampedusa and Licy lived in a rented room in Piazza Castelnuovo in Palermo. Times were hard: the city had been destroyed, inflation was rampant, many people were poor, homeless and living in misery. Licy threw herself into her psychoanalytic studies. She often travelled to Rome, and started practising and teaching in Palermo. Lampedusa was once again involved in the on-going family succession feuds over the division of his great-grandfather's estate. In November 1945, an agreement was finally reached. The second floor of a building in Via Butera 42 was allotted half to Lampedusa and half to his cousin Carolina. Lampedusa moved in, though the place was in a terrible state of disrepair.

In 1950, the first and second floor of the adjoining building were put on sale. The whole building had once been the property of the Lampedusas, but in 1865 half of it had been sold to the shipbroker De Pace. Lampedusa now bought back part of the De Pace property on a mortgage. Licy had left him alone in Palermo. With a broken heart, he managed to move from his childhood home to the building in Via Butera. Throughout 1951, he dealt with co-inheritors, banks and lawyers, overseeing the necessary restoration of the building.

In the meantime, there was not enough money to pay back the mortgage, something Lampedusa would hide from his wife to his death. Yet, despite his financial troubles, some rewards awaited. In 1944 Lampedusa was selected to be the president of the provincial and eventually the regional Red Cross. He stayed in charge until 1947, fulfilling his role with zeal.

In the Fifties, Lampedusa seemed to have regained his balance: his interest in literature revived, and he was no longer dependent on his mother or his wife. Alongside some friends, he began to frequent the house of Bebbuzzo Sgadari di Lo Monaco, a music critic and great lover of culture. His home was a meeting place for all intellectuals coming through Palermo. It was here that Lampedusa and Lucio Piccolo met their third cousin, Gioacchino Lanza, who later became Lampedusa's adopted son. By 1953 they were close friends.

In 1953, Lampedusa offered to teach English language and literature to Francesco Orlando, then a law student. They started with language lessons three times a week in the living room of the first floor of Via Butera. Soon enough they moved on to literature. At the beginning of the course, Lampedusa was surrounded by a small group of followers, who attended fairly regularly up to the time when he reached Shakespeare. Then they slowly lost interest – until they all reappeared when he covered Eliot and Joyce in the summer of 1954. Between the autumn of 1953 and September 1954, Lampedusa wrote by hand about a thousand pages, which were to become his *English Literature*, finally published by Mondadori in 1990–91.

After the English course ended in 1954, Lampedusa set out to draw one up in French literature. This was never as complete as the English one, but there are nonetheless some five hundred pages in his minute handwriting. Originally, both courses had been created after Francesco Orlando had decided to abandon law in order to dedicate himself to literature. Orlando later wrote in his *Memories of Lampedusa* that the author seemed to have gradually lost interest in his relationship with his pupil. Throughout the winter and spring of 1955, he was already working on *The Leopard*.

Lampedusa may have been motivated in part from the emergence of Lucio Piccolo as a poet himself. In 1954, Lucio's mother Teresa had died, leaving Lucio free to dedicate himself to his interests. Before then his main passion had been music: he had been a talented musician, a connoisseur of Wagner, and had been composing a Magnificat for the last thirty years, though in the Thirties his musical career had come to a sort of standstill. After his mother's death, however, the verses came thick and fast, and he published a small volume at his own expense in 1954, entitled *9 liriche* (*9 Poems*). This volume was sent to Eugenio Montale, with a letter of introduction from Lampedusa, but the wrong postage was paid. Montale would later claim that he read the volume especially because he'd paid 180-lire excess to receive it. In any case, he was impressed and invited Lucio to attend a forum where established authors would introduce emerging or unknown ones. Lampedusa accompanied his cousin.

Apparently, the idea of writing a novel about his great-grandfather was one he had entertained for a long time. The original plan was to write a novel taking place over the course of twenty-four hours – just like Joyce's *Ulysses* – as attested by the first part of the novel. In June 1955 the story had already been drafted and edited several times, when Lampedusa set it aside to write *Ricordi d'infanzia*, a collection of his childhood memories. These writings would contribute significantly to the central chapters of *The Leopard*, which thus extended beyond the scope of its Joycean roots.

Moreover, two visits to Palma di Montechiaro – the ancient feudal town of the Lampedusas – in the summer and the autumn of 1955, also proved a strong influence and inspiration. The town had been founded by twin brothers

Carlo and Giulio Tomasi on 3rd May 1637, and in the following years had been imbued with familial religious zeal. Having become a duke, Carlo renounced worldly life to become a Theatine monk. The title and fiefdom went to his twin Giulio, who in 1659 bequeathed his palace to the Monastery of SS. Rosario, where his four daughters and later his wife all took monastic vows. Giulio's firstborn, Giuseppe, followed in the footsteps of his uncle and became a Theatine; he was later sanctified. His sister Isabella, too, who had taken the name of Maria Crocifissa, was one of the great mystics of seventeenth-century Sicily.

This saintly family history was somewhat obscured by the ensuing family feuds over inheritance. Nonetheless, when Lampedusa visited Palma in August 1955 for the first time, he was extremely taken with the place. Upon his return to Palermo he enthusiastically organized a second visit along with Licy, Gioacchino Lanza and his fiancée.

On 24th May 1956, a first version of the novel, in four parts, was sent by Lucio Piccolo to Count Federici, a representative of Mondadori with whom he had been in touch. In the meantime, the novel was still developing – a new chapter was sent to Federici on 10th October. On 10th December, however, the novel, now in six parts, was rejected. Lampedusa was greatly disappointed, but writing was now his life, and he did not get discouraged.

In the last few months of his life, from the autumn of 1956 to the winter of 1957, Lampedusa wrote another two chapters of *The Leopard*. Between January and February 1957, he set down the novel on paper once more: it was now in eight parts. He also wrote two stories: one short, *Joy and the Law,* towards the end of 1956, and a longer one, *The Siren,* in the winter of 1957. That same winter he also started a new novel, *The Blind Kittens*, of which we only have the first chapter.

In December 1956, the adoption of Gioacchino Lanza went through. Aside from some financial difficulties, everything seemed to be going well. In February 1957, the manuscript of *The Leopard* was sent to the novelist Elio Vittorini, who worked as an editor at Einaudi. At the same time, a patient of Licy's, Giorgio Giargia, had offered to show it to Elena Croce, the daughter of Benedetto Croce, and a lady of great cultural influence. This last contact would be the path to publication.

In April 1957, Tomasi was diagnosed with lung cancer. Although he had suffered from a few recurring illnesses, complaining especially of smoker's cough and a limp due to his rheumatism, there was no hint of his final illness until he started coughing up blood. A tumour in his right lung was found. In late May he went to Rome to have it removed, but the cancer was too far advanced. He was advised against the operation due to the state of his lungs and the position of the tumour. He tried cobalt therapy, but died on the 23rd July.

He left behind letters for both his wife and his adoptive son. In them, he asked them to pursue the publication of his novel, though he insisted it should not be at their expense. On 2nd July he had received a letter from Vittorini, who had read and in his turn rejected the novel on behalf of Einaudi, mostly on ideological grounds. In the end, *The Leopard* was published posthumously by Feltrinelli in November 1958, after Elena Croce signalled it to the novelist and editor Giorgio Bassani. The following year it won the Premio Strega, the most prestigious Italian literary award, and has since then become an international bestseller and a universally recognized twentieth-century classic.

ACKNOWLEDGEMENTS

The publisher wishes to thank Gioacchino Lanza Tomasi for his assistance and support in the production of this volume. A special thanks also goes to Costanza Scarpa and Natalie de Pointis Brighty for their editorial help, and to the Erede family for their permission to reproduce the text of Lampedusa's postcards and letters to Massimo Erede.

All the pictures in this volume– with the exception of the photo of Casimiro Piccolo, which is reproduced courtesy of Enzo Sellerio Editore – have been reproduced by kind permission of Gioacchino Lanza Tomasi.